CW00553123

VW
POWER AND STYLE

This book is dedicated to
Gordon Cruickshank,
a man of courage in the face of adversity

VW POWER AND STYLE

IAN KUAH

MRP

MOTOR RACING PUBLICATIONS LIMITED
Unit 6, The Pilton Estate, 46 Pitlake, Croydon CR0 3RY, England

First published 1991

British Library Cataloguing in Publication Data
Kuah, Ian
  VW power and style.
  1. Cars. Maintenance & repair
  I. Title
  629.28722

  ISBN 0-947981-49-7

Photoset in Great Britain by
Tek-Art Ltd, West Wickham, Kent

Printed and bound in Hong Kong by
Bookbuilders Ltd

Contents

Introduction

The Volkswagen Golf GTI is more than just a cult car, it is both a contemporary classic and an international phenomenon. Although history tells of compact high-performance cars like the Mini-Cooper S, the NSU Prinz TT and the BMW 2002Tii that were the nemesis of larger, more powerful machinery on both road and track, no other car has inspired aftermarket personalization on the scale that has been seen among Golf GTI owners almost from day one.

No other affordable car has been as sought after for its badge image, either. Volkswagen must sorely regret not having taken out a trademark copyright on the title GTI. But the real thing is indeed a GTI; any imitator is usually only described as a GTi.

The key word in the GTI's success story is 'international', for not only was this new-generation VW the progenitor of the so-called 'hot-hatchback' craze, but its status as a cult car has followed it into every single market where Volkswagen has put it on sale, whether through importation or local production. Perhaps it is fitting that it should have come from Volkswagen, for its ancestor the Beetle, in its own very different style, was truly a world car too.

The GTI's official birth in September 1975 also contributed greatly to another German phenomenon which has spread to many cars, either straight from the factory or through the aftermarket – the body styling kit. The handful of engineers in Volkswagen's prototype department who secretly worked on the 'Sport Golf' out-of-

hours while developing the basic Golf production car could not have had any inkling of just how far-reaching would be the consequences of their enthusiasm to both the high-performance car world and the accessories business.

It would be unfair, however, if the Golf GTI alone were to take all the credit for bringing new and repeat owners into the Volkswagen realm of power and style. There are many who, perhaps for reasons of work, need a stylish four-door saloon and others who value the individual but practical formula of a hatchback coupe. And there are the lucky few who can afford to indulge themselves in open-air motoring. For these customers, the engines and floorpans of the Golf GTI Mk1 and Mk2 form the basis of the Jetta, Scirocco, Corrado and Golf GTI Cabriolet variations, cars which have also received considerable attention from aftermarket tuners. Enthusiasts' cars in their own right, these variants have created their own following in the various countries in which they are sold and, as with the Golf GTI, there are clubs that cater for them either collectively or individually, for example the Scirocco clubs in Holland and Germany.

The high-performance fuel-injected Volkswagens are a phenomenon of the last 16 years. They have created a new market sector, a whole aftermarket industry and a new kind of car enthusiast. The fact that one formula of motorcar can appeal so strongly to buyers from such diverse cultures as America, Australia, Britain, France, Germany, Greece, Italy, Japan, Singapore and

South Africa endorses the rightness of the basic concept. Each major country in which the GTI is sold has largely developed its own tuning industry based on the indigenous culture and automobile engineering heritage of its people.

The diversity of products which has emanated from all these conversion and tuning specialists has enabled me to offer a new kind of car enthusiast's book, one which examines first of all these cars which are one of the most notable motoring successes of the late 20th century and then the many interpretations provided by tuners who have worked so well on the basic theme, to the delight of performance-minded VW enthusiasts throughout the world.

Acknowledgements
There are many knowledgeable and very helpful people all over the world who have each contributed in some way to the information and illustrations that appear in these pages. I would like to dedicate this book to all of them with a big thank you, and apologise to any I may have inadvertently missed.

In Germany: Christa Resow of the VW Auto-Museum in Wolfsburg; Brigitte Seitz, PR Manager VW Motorsport; Reinhard Jühe of Wilhelm Karmann GmbH; and all the tuning firms who contributed information and photos.

In the UK: Laura Warren, Paul Buckett, Edward Rowe and Beverley Gale of the Press and PR Department of VAG (UK) Ltd for their support in this project, and a special vote of thanks to David Bryant and Chris Trouse of the VAG (UK) Ltd Photographic Unit for access to their archives.

Outside the official network, I would like to extend my gratitude to Brian Ricketts of BR Motorsport, who has reinforced my view that he is Britain's leading GTI guru. I am also grateful for the kind assistance of Mike and Stephanie Kingdon of the GTI Drivers' Club, and David Pipes and Graham Whittaker of Club GTI.

In South Africa: Chris Lourens, GTi Club of South Africa; Alan Clunnie, PR Manager VWSA, for his untiring efforts to collate the history of the car in his country.

In the USA: Jay Amestoy jr, former PR Manager, VW of America. A big thank you to Darrell Vittone of Techtonics Tuning in Riverside, Aaron Neumann of Automotive Performance Systems in Anaheim and Ron Moser of AutoTech in Aliso Viejo, the three top VW tuners in Southern California.

Last but not least, I would like to thank John Blunsden of MRP for spotting the seed of my idea and allowing it to germinate, and Jane Marshall for tirelessly reading the script.

Ian Kuah

1

GTI: formula phenomenal

In the early 1970s, the sales and marketing departments of the major German car manufacturers lacked the keen edge they have today. Relatively, times were easy. The tip of the Japanese iceberg had only just begun to emerge, and the oil crisis, though looming, had not yet bittten deep. In Stuttgart, at Porsche, the development department wanted sales and marketing to put 500 of the 911 Carrera RS 2.7 cars through their dealer network so that the car could be homologated for Group 4 GT racing. Sales considered this no more than a nuisance and were rather surprised when the cars were sold very quickly. Another 500 were made for the 1973 model year to make the car eligible for Group 3 racing and these went quickly too. And the demand continued.

The oil crisis later that year dampened the performance car market if only because social responsibility in terms of fuel conservation suddenly became a big issue. Over at Volkswagen, the Golf was launched in early 1974, just at the right time to become a sales success as a compact and economical family car in the new climate. In May 1975, the 'Sport Golf' which a handful of development engineers had worked on as their pet project out of official hours, became an officially sanctioned project.

To boost the image of the company, it was decided to homologate the car for Group 1 Production Touring Car racing. This meant that 5,000 cars would have to pass through dealer showrooms. As with Porsche, the sales and marketing division were not happy and reluctantly backed the production of the car on the understanding that only 5,000 units would be made. They calculated that if these cars were divided amongst all the VW dealers in Europe, it would not be difficult to get rid of them quickly and forget the whole matter. But fate took a hand in the proceedings. The customers who saw this discreet looking performance machine in the showrooms asked questions, took a test drive and bought the car. They told their friends, and soon VW were in the embarrassing position of being back ordered for cars they almost could not supply. Quite simply, the public had been starved of high performance cars through the oil crisis and its immediate aftermath, and if they could now have a small, fuel-efficient Volkswagen hatchback with the performance of a 2.8-litre Mercedes or BMW and for half the price, then that was what they wanted. It was not too long before VW found themselves making 5,000 cars a month to satisfy demand. Quite unwittingly, sales and marketing found that they had abetted the birth of a car that would not only in due course influence every other major manufacturer in Europe and Japan, but also alter the direction of the aftermarket tuning industry across the face of the globe.

Before the Golf GTI, the 'hot hatchback' did not exist. Small fast cars were Mini-Coopers and Fiat Abarths and if you went one size up there was the Renault Gordini and the NSU Prinz TT. Between these nimble machines and the big autobahn stormers from BMW and Mercedes were high-performance small saloons like the BMW 2002, Alfa Romeo Giulia and Fiat 124ST.

The basic Golf itself was not an entirely clear concept from the start. In the late 1960s, it had become evident that the Beetle's days were numbered. A car that had been in production

Project EA 276, seen here in the VW museum, was a milestone in the transition from Beetle to Golf. Already established is the front-wheel-drive hatchback format.

A pre-production GTI. Note the experimental grille badge, the style of which was revised before production began, and the small front spoiler.

In its final pre-production form, with revised badge and spoiler, this GTI is being hammered round a race circuit during handling trials.

Rear view of a pre-production car showing early sheet-metalwork in the number-plate area which was subsequently changed in design.

since the end of WW2, it was a great success story but now looking old and tired apart from lacking the performance and cabin space of newer rivals. The EA 276 project of 1969 was the first step in the direction of the Golf. This car was not yet a Golf but several steps away from the Beetle. It did however embody many of the elements that characterized the new generation of VW as the company saw it. It had a front engine driving the front wheels, a short rear overhang with a long roofline, a large rear hatch and linked trailing arm rear suspension. The engine was initially the four-cylinder air-cooled boxer engine from the Beetle.

Later that year, the concept was altered to define the need for a water-cooled transversely mounted four-cylinder engine.

At the 1969 Turin Motor Show, VW's Chairman, Kurt Lotz chose six cars which he found to be interesting and, on further investigation, it transpired that four of those six were designed by Giorgetto Giugiaro. Lotz set up a meeting with the Italian designer and asked him to produce a new passenger car design for VW. In fact, VW wanted him to design two new cars, one medium-sized vehicle which became the Passat and one to replace the Beetle. Soon after the contract was signed, VW's chairmanship was taken over by Rudolf Leiding from Audi, and the design of the car later known as the Golf went through difficult times. Leiding was noted for his prudence and was hesitant to switch from the Beetle to a new car of such radically different concept. But finally the Golf was born in a form not too far removed from Giugiaro's original.

Rudolph Leiding had been the boss at Auto-Union prior to that company's takeover by VW. The head of Auto-Union's technical department was Ludwig Kraus and in the new order of things he was absorbed into Audi where he and his team penned the Audi 80 and a new family of engines known as the Type 827 to power it. This was a belt-driven single overhead camshaft design with a cast iron block and light alloy head. Two engine sizes, 1,296cc and 1,471cc, were productionized and both were mounted in-line with the gearbox behind. The basic floorpan and mechanicals were then grafted under a new VW bodyshell which had been designed by Giugiaro. This was launched in 1973 as the Passat and took VW into a totally new area of the market.

By this time, the new small VW was nearly ready and Giugiaro had come up with both a three or five-door hatchback saloon and a three-door coupe design on the same floorpan powered by the Type 827 engine mounted transversely across the front. Still smarting from the VW K70 fiasco, the company could not afford to make any mistakes and so elected to launch the Karmann-built low-volume Scirocco coupe in early 1974 and hold back the Wolfsburg-built Golf till June.

The chassis of the new car was very advanced for the time and had several novel features. While the MacPherson strut front suspension was a design that had been proven on other makes of car before, the rear axle was a torsion beam with trailing arms and coil springs with concentrically mounted dampers. The combination proved very effective and endowed the car with a very good ride and sharp handling helped also by rack-and-pinion steering. It was enthusiastic feedback from the press and customers on the sporty handling and performance of the new car that finally awoke the sales and marketing people to the possibilities of a Sport Golf. On that basis, the green light was given to the project and not long after that it received its 'GTI' title. GT, short for Gran Turismo in Italian, was already a popular suffix for sporting derivatives of family saloons, but no one at VW seems to be able to account for the 'I'. The German for 'injection' is 'Einspritzung',

Close cousins. Based on the same running gear, the Golf and Scirocco show their different personalities. Both shapes came from the Giugiaro studio.

hence the 'E' in Opel's GT/E cars, so it did not come from the fact that the final production engine was fuel-injected – unless it was an extension of the Italian influence, 'I' for 'iniezione'.

At the start of the programme, the first prototype GTI had a 1,588cc engine with a Solex twin-choke carburettor and 100bhp. It was straight out of the Audi 80GT. The car performed well but the engineers felt that they could do better and with the full resources of the company now behind them, began development to create a high-performance version of the Type 827 engine that had already been modified for the Bosch K-Jetronic fuel-injection system to enable it to meet US emission laws. They found an extra 10bhp by doing this but also improved drivability and enhanced fuel economy at the same time. The uprated engine then completed the circle of events by ending up also under the bonnet of the car it had been borrowed from, in a derivative of the Audi 80 quite logically called the 80GTE.

Initial thoughts on the cabin furnishings for the Golf GTI were angled towards a fairly basic car that would appeal to young enthusiast drivers. It soon became apparent though that the car would also appeal to older well-heeled buyers who wanted a town car with a bit of style or just a small fast car that would be socially acceptable in the new economy-conscious era. The emphasis thus swung towards high quality furnishings. Externally, the car grew a bigger front spoiler to aid stability at speed, and tests proved that adding ventilated front discs was enough to provide the stopping power required. The chassis modifications took the form of uprated springs and dampers and an anti-roll bar at the rear. This bar was particularly clever in its application as it was simply bolted through the trailing arms of the torsion beam and needed no body mounting.

Because no such car had ever been produced before, the sales people had little say in the ultimate specification. The engineers developed the car more or less as they felt it ought to be done and now recall with pride that not a single item they added in the transformation from 'Golf ordinaire' to GTI was removed by the Board before the car made its public debut. The GTI was first shown at the 1975 Frankfurt Show, but it was nine months before you could buy a production car. Six prototypes had been made before the car was officially sanctioned and 15 durability test cars were subsequently made up. These were mercilessly pounded in the search for weaknesses,

The interior of the early GTI had overtly sporting overtones. The cabin was nicely finished for a small car in the mid-1970s. Note the golf-ball gear knob.

Plastic-covered bumpers extended round to the wheelarches gave the 1978 Golf more visual appeal as well as better protection.

one such car covering 62,000 miles, half of this being high speed running on the autobahns. The prototypes were baked in North Africa and frozen in Scandinavia to make sure that no development work was later done by customers.

The sterling work of the development team that had expanded from four or five to over 100 in a year showed in a car that was lean and agile with no excess flab. It was fast, tractable and comfortable, and it handled magnificently. And it was discreet, a true engineer's car devoid of any fancy frills. The power-to-weight ratio was an excellent 105bhp/ton. The engineers say that it was the Golf's compact dimensions and basically sporting engine and chassis that made the car so amenable to the GTI treatment. The smaller and larger cars in the VW range would not have been suitable. Based on the same mechanicals, the Scirocco GTI comes close, but you have to trade more overtly sporting looks for less accommodation and a higher price tag.

The GTI logo on the front grille went through a change before the familiar upright serif typeface was adopted for production versions. Early cars were distinguished from their lesser brethren only by a red outline to the grille, wider wheels (still in steel at that stage), side stripes, black decal trim around the rear window and the GTI badging on the front grille and rear hatch. Thus, the GTI was difficult to tell from its more tame stablemate at a distance, and was something of a Q-car that caused red faces amongst drivers of larger cars as the cheeky little VW flashed them out of the way on the autobahn and then disappeared into the distance.

The interior of the early GTI had check-patterned Recaro-style seats with separate headrests. These gave good support to occupants when the car was being driven 'properly'. A matching rev counter went in beside the speed-ometer and a slim centre console was added which housed an oil temperature gauge and a clock. A three-spoke sports steering wheel with the Wolfsburg crest in the middle put the finishing touch to the interior package.

A change in external appearance took place in 1978 when the girder-like bumpers of the early Golfs gave way to more modern and elegant wrap-around plastic units which, apart from looking better, also gave better parking bump protection. At this time, UK-bound GTIs started to come in with the Audi 80/Passat type of alloy wheels as standard. These were still an option on the Continent, where equipment levels differ.

The definitive GTI 1.6 was the 1982 model with its nine-spoke alloy wheels and wind deflectors on the A-pillars.

The French got this 136bhp GTI 16S with Oettinger-developed engine and BBS body kit. They had to pay 50% more for it, though.

A four-speed gearbox and a small capacity high-revving engine have never been a recipe for either optimum acceleration or relaxed cruising, so in 1979, the GTI gained a five-speed close-ratio gearbox. Acceleration through the gears was aided by the well chosen ratios of this box, each gear taking up perfectly where the last one left off, giving a stimulating continuous blast of acceleration. The time for the 0-60mph sprint dropped by almost a second to 8.5 seconds and top speed was notched up slightly from 111mph to 113mph.

The 1981 model year brought with it a significant change to the interior of the GTI with new striped seat cover material that was both more modern and more tasteful than the rather lurid checks. Accompanying this was a complete redesign of the facia and instrument panel that would set the design of VW instruments into the 1990s. The speedometer and rev counter were now housed under a single non-reflective plastic cover with the fuel and water temperature gauges, digital LCD clock and a battery of warning lights in between. The centre console was also widened with a blank panel added that could house three extra instruments. These cars also had a rather garish red stripe around the facia to mirror the purposeful one on the grille. Externally, the car gained larger tail-light clusters.

A certain amount of evolution was now taking place every model year, and the next round of changes for 1982 brought a new design of alloy wheel with nine spokes, plastic rain deflectors for the A-pillars, combined armrest/door pulls and door pockets with grilles for small oval speakers. The red stripe around the facia was deleted.

GTI 16S

In the meantime, the opposition had not been idle, and despite its widely publicized suspension problems and lack of general engine refinement, the carburettor-equipped Ford Escort XR3 had been gaining ground on the now five-year-old GTI. Other new cars such as the Renault 5 Gordini were also threatening to upset the status quo, particularly in France, a very important market for the GTI with 50% of Golf sales being the sporty model. For the French division of VW, it was vital that the GTI should remain the market leader. The factory had been experimenting with turbocharging and found that while it was easy to get upwards of 150bhp, the high underbonnet temperatures (with both inlet and exhaust at the back of the engine) and high fuel consumption made it an impractical idea.

The solution for VW in France came in the

Available on the Continent in both 1.6 and 1.8-litre versions, the five-door GTI Mk1 was never sold in Britain or America.

form of the Okrasa 16-valve cylinder head which Oettinger had been developing as an aftermarket conversion kit for the Golf. Oettinger had been tuning VWs for more than 30 years and their twin-cam crossflow head appeared in the late 1970s as the growing GTI following brought with it a demand for ways of improving the standard product. Oettinger's engine retained the cogged-belt drive to one camshaft, with the second camshaft gear-driven from the first. Experience with this unit was to play an important part in the development of VW's own 16-valve head later.

The Oettinger head was designed to bolt straight on to the 1.6-litre engine. Even so, long term reliability was looked at properly and new forged pistons were fitted to suit the new combustion chamber shape and increase reliability. Compression ratio was now 10.5:1. The crankshaft and connecting rods were balanced and the oil pump uprated to cope with higher lubrication demands. A light alloy sump with intricate baffling to keep the oil from surging in high-g cornering was fitted. With an uprated K-Jetronic fuel system, the power output rose to 136bhp at 6,500rpm and torque went up from the stock 101lb/ft at 5,000rpm to 116lb/ft at 5,500rpm.

Oettinger pronounced the engine good for 8,000rpm, while not advocating exceeding 7,000rpm too often, and fitted a lower final drive (4.17:1) to allow it to pull 7,000rpm in top. At those revs, the car would do a genuine 121mph on 185/60HR14 tyres. They chose Uniroyal rubber and 6J x 14 ATS alloy wheels. The uprating job was completed by adding a lower wishbone strut brace to the front suspension and specifying fast road brake pads. Cosmetically, these cars were altered by the addition of a BBS body kit, the Hella four-headlamp grille and 16S badges ('soupapes' is French for valves).

Up to this point, any customer could buy an Oettinger conversion, but with the idea of selling complete cars through VW dealers in France, the car had to undergo extensive tests at the factory. It passed these tests and gained the benefit of the full VW dealer warranty. The factory in Wolfsburg were particularly keen on the car because, after 400 were made, they could homologate the 16-valve engine for Group 4 competition. The arrangement was that VW would supply complete Golf GTIs to Oettinger who would modify the engines and return the unused parts – cylinder heads, pistons etc.

With a 0-60mph time of 7.4 seconds, the 16S was the full measure of the opposition, even the Renault 5 turbo of its day and indeed the later Fiat

Underbonnet layout of the GTI Mk1, in the version launched for the 1983 model year. Enlarging the capacity to 1.8 litres provided 112bhp and 109lb/ft to help VW fight the hot-hatchback war.

The dashboard of the 1.8-litre version was distinguished by a temperature gauge and MFA computer.

Strada Abarth 2-litre, but it cost 50% more than a standard 1,600cc GTI.

GTI 1.8 litre

For Wolfsburg, the cheapest and easiest way to answer the threat from the mounting opposition was to fall back on the age-old adage, 'there is no substitute for cubic inches'. With the release of the Ford Escort XR3i and RS1600i imminent, in the autumn of 1982, VW wheeled out their new weapon in the fight to retain the 'best hot hatch' crown. From the Wolfsburg armoury came the

Golf GTI 1.8. Although on paper the 1,781cc motor with its 81.0mm x 86.4mm bore and stroke (up from 79.5mm x 80.0mm) gained only 2bhp and 8lb/ft of torque, it was a classic case of 'it's not what you do but the way that you do it'. The new engine produced its maximum torque at 3,500rpm instead of 4,800rpm, while maximum power was produced a less significant 300 revs lower at 5,800rpm. This long-stroke motor was the first step in a gradual progression towards lower-revving, more torquey power units that we will see continue over the years in the GTI's life.

The engine used a different block of the same basic design, but the cylinder head and pistons were completely new. The 1.6-litre GTI engine had a flat head and bowl-in-piston combustion chambers. The 1.8-litre unit had most of the combustion chamber in the head and only part of it in the piston top. Many aftermarket tuners, concerned mostly with top-end power, prefer the earlier design. The effect of the change was significantly in favour of low and mid-range torque however. The rival XR3i and Astra/Kadett GTE were able to match the new GTI 1.8 through the gears from a standing start and even edge it out slightly in top speed through better aerodynamics, but they lacked the smooth and gutsy power delivery and consequent flexibility in the higher gears at low crankshaft speeds.

The altered characteristics of the GTI's engine translated into more effortless acceleration and, coupled with a slightly taller final drive (3.89:1 instead of 3.70:1), gave the car superior ground-covering ability with greater refinement. The close-ratio five-speed gearbox which was so well suited to the 1.6-litre model was an equally good partner for the bigger engine – indeed, from the fuel economy point of view it was even better. Petrol is wasted with every gearchange, and if you are driving for maximum efficiency it is prudent to keep close to the peak of the torque curve: so much the better if there is lots of torque low down. Driven this way, the bigger engine actually extended the car's range on the same small 8.9-gallon fuel tank. Interior changes for the new model were confined to the addition of a stalk-operated multi-function computer and a temperature gauge.

Campaign Golf GTI

In 1983, with the life of the Mk1 Golf drawing to a close, Wolfsburg produced a limited-edition model to boost sales of the GTI in the face of competition from the XR3i and Kadett GTE. They launched the car that has become known as the Campaign Golf, which featured a steel sliding sunroof, four-headlamp grille and 6J x 14in Pirelli alloy wheels shod with 185/60HR14 P6 tyres. On the Continent these cars had wheelarch spats and bumper ends finished in the body colour, leaving just the centre part black, while UK-bound cars retained the all-black bumpers of the normal GTI. These Campaign GTIs are much sought after by enthusiasts looking for a late Mk1 car.

Rabbit GTI

In the United States, the Golf was renamed the Rabbit to bestow the image of a small and fast runner. To make the Rabbit cheaper to sell against domestic sub-compact cars and the imported Japanese hordes, VW set up a manufacturing plant in Westmoreland County, Pennsylvania. US-spec Rabbits had been equipped with fuel injection to meet the emission laws ever since they were sold in the US and by the time the first GTI version of the Rabbit was due to roll off the assembly line in Westmoreland for the 1983 model year, the standard 1,715cc Rabbit was only making 75bhp at 6,100rpm and 89lb/ft of torque. This was a long way short of the 110bhp and 101lb/ft of the European GTI.

Prior to this, the need for a sports model had given birth to the Rabbit S, which had the European GTI suspension and sports seats but the normal engine of the US version. US Rabbits had already departed from their German cousins with a locally styled dashboard and instrument panel, and customer discontent grew as the now better-handling Rabbit S merely underlined the extra weight and low power of the car.

The Canadians had been slightly better off. VW of Canada had started to import the German-built GTI in 1978 and it had the full Euro GTI chassis specification apart from using US-style impact bumpers and 5J x 13in steel wheels shod with 175/70SR13 tyres. Alloys were optional. Its engine, though, was just the US emission-spec 1,471cc unit with 71bhp at 5,800rpm and 73lb/ft of torque at 3,500rpm. It was a bunny with its teeth pulled. The start-up at Westmoreland in 1980 effectively stopped the importation of the German-made GTI to Canada and after that year, if you wanted a German-built VW, you had to buy a Rabbit Convertible, a Jetta or a Scirocco. With less strict emission laws, the Canadians had slightly more powerful engines with 76bhp at 5,000rpm and 91.3lb/ft of torque at 3,000rpm.

The cries for a proper Rabbit GTI were heard at VW of America and a GTI team was set up under Duane Miller, VWOA's Vice President of Engineering. The timing was fortuitous for at that time two events in Germany conspired to supply the necessary hardware. The first of these was the introduction of 14in diameter alloy wheels for the Quantum (Passat) that would also fit the Rabbit and the other was the development of a US-spec version of the 1.8-litre high-performance engine meant for the Euro Golf GTI. With these two vital ingredients in the melting pot, the VWOA engineers set about making a real Rabbit GTI.

The US Rabbit is nearly 200lb heavier than its European counterpart, no thanks to heavy hardware like 5mph impact bumpers, emission controls and air conditioning. To use the exact suspension of the Euro GTI would therefore have been inappropriate. The front spring rates were increased by 22% over the 1982 Rabbit and the rears changed from progressive to linear, ending up 29% stiffer. The dampers were also uprated using the MacPherson struts from the Euro GTI. These gave two thirds more rebound control than the standard Rabbit's. Fine tuning was done as per the Golf GTI with front and rear anti-roll bars, and the 6J x 14 alloy wheels were shod with 185/60HR14 Pirelli P6s.

By the 1982 model year, the ordinary 1,715cc Rabbit engine had crept up to 74bhp at 5,000rpm

First of the factory special editions was the Campaign GTI. This is the Continental version with colour-coded wheelarch extensions and bumpers: for Britain these appendages remained black. Alloy wheels featured P for Pirelli cutouts.

The American-built Rabbit 'S' of 1981 had a different front grille and sidelights, as well as clumsy impact bumpers. It was more show than go.

Trendsetting Golf Cabriolet. This is a US-market version, exported from Europe: only the basic saloon was manufactured in the States.

and 94lb/ft of torque at 3,000rpm. With the new 1,781cc engine in the Rabbit GTI, power rose dramatically to 90bhp at 5,500rpm and torque was now a respectable 105lb/ft at 3,250rpm. Compression ratio was 8.5:1 compared to 8.2:1 on the standard car. Electronic ignition and digital idling stabilization continued to be used along with the Bosch K-Jetronic fuel-injection. The exhaust system was also revised with a freer flowing, larger diameter pipe and redesigned catalytic convertor: back pressure was reduced by 35%. The close-ratio five-speed gearbox was brought into play but with a 3.94:1 final drive rather than the 3.89:1 of the standard 1982 Rabbit which was the same as that of the Euro GTI 1.6. 0-60mph was accomplished in 10.0 seconds and top speed was 104mph.

Going topless

After the classic Karmann-built Beetle Cabriolet, it was logical that the successor to the Beetle should also get a soft-top. Karmann made the prototype in 1976 and the car was officially announced at the 1979 Geneva Show. Cutting the

roof off a modern monocoque vehicle seriously compromises the structure. To regain the necessary stiffness, Karmann added cross-members and reinforcements along the sills. If you peer under the car you can see these reinforcements running the length of the car between the wheel arches, and they are welded to the inner wings. A roll-over bar is welded both to the stiffening sill and the sheet metal of the car and a crossmember is welded under the dashboard. The luggage area within the small boot is contained in a sheet metal box that braces the rear of the car. The bonnet, front wings and doors were carried over from the hatchback but all the other panels were made specifically for the convertible.

The Karmann-built Golf was more than your average rag-top car. Its soft, folding top was a work of art in itself. With a substantial steel frame and two fabric layers, the hood even had a glass rear window with a demister facility. Lowering or raising the hood was an absolute doddle: single-handed, you could do it within a minute once practised. All you had to do to lower it was release

The darkened areas in this illustration show the structural reinforcement engineered into the Cabriolet shell to make it acceptably rigid.

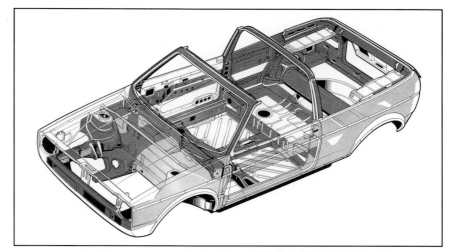

Special editions of the Cabriolet were very popular. Despite being very difficult to keep pristine, the all-white version was a favourite.

The Cabriolet's folding top was of complex, double-layer construction to ensure saloon-like protection when closed, and included a glass rear window.

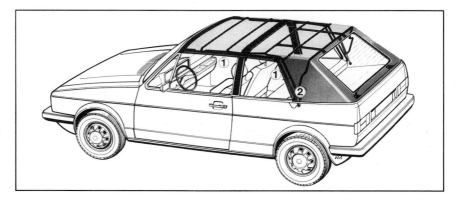

21

Later Cabriolets like this 1988 version had side skirts and one-piece bumpers. The open model remained Mk1-based even after the advent of the Mk2 saloon.

the two handles above the windscreen and push the hood back, where it folded neatly into a pile. If you were going to drive fast, it was advisable to button the canvas cover on to protect the edges. Raising it again involved pressing the safety release catch and then swinging the hood over the screen, releasing the handles and then pulling them taut again. The securing handles had a screw adjuster system built in so you could compensate for hood fabric movement when re-engaging the hooks in their screen-top locations. Simple and elegant. In winter, with the hood up and the heater going, this double-layered covering was as snug as a hatchback. For the 1990 model year, the Golf Cabriolet acquired a power-operated hood as standard. Now all you have to do is release the roof clamps and press a button to experience the advantages of an open car.

Making the Cabriolet acceptably rigid created a weight penalty however, and the open Golf ended up 300lb heavier than the hatchback with a high proportion of that weight in the rear. The suspension settings had to be changed to cope and of course the car was not as accelerative or as fast all-out.

Golf 2

The Golf Mk1 was a hard act to follow – VW's rivals had found that out. But now the pace-setters themselves had substantially to improve the recipe if they were to remain competitive into the 1990s. Through the late 1970s and into the early 1980s, VW's own, in-house design team had been gathering pace and their first major contribution in the decade was the Scirocco 2. For the new Golf, submissions from two outside consultants including Giugiaro were invited, and after studying the reactions of a group of 500 invited participants at customer clinics, VW opted for its own design.

The design brief had been quite rigorous. The original car, nine years down the line, had recaptured its best-seller title from the Opel Kadett in Germany and compared to all the newer rivals in its class had only two major shortcomings. These were inadequate rear legroom and luggage capacity. Solving these problems in a new design was relatively straightforward, but the bigger question facing the engineers and stylists was the shape the new car would take. The year before, Audi and Ford had respectively launched their 100 Series and Sierra, both cars showing different degrees of daring in aerodynamics and overall

The Mk2 Golf, here in two-door GTI form, was larger and more rounded than its predecessor, though retaining a recognizable family likeness. It was designed in-house by VW.

Facia layout of the Mk2 continued the simple, functional theme of the earlier car but gathered the minor controls together more neatly.

form. The two cars had gone down well in Germany, but the British initially did not like the 'jelly mould' shape of the Sierra. VW had to tread carefully. Their choice was between a radical, smooth, rounded shape resembling the Auto 2000 research vehicle shown at Frankfurt in 1981 (much of which has since surfaced in the 1988 Passat) or the basic form of the original Golf, stretched and rounded off.

The latter route was chosen, leaving no doubt as to the antecedents of the car. Golf 2 was 6.8in longer, incorporating a 2.8in longer wheelbase, and 2in wider. Using the contoured inner door panels pioneered on the Scirocco 2, 3.5in of extra elbow room was found. The basic similarity of shapes belied the dramatic improvement in drag coefficient. The tumble from 0.42 to 0.34, even multiplied by a slightly increased frontal area, still added up to a 17% improvement. Detailing was particularly neat with recessed rain gutters and

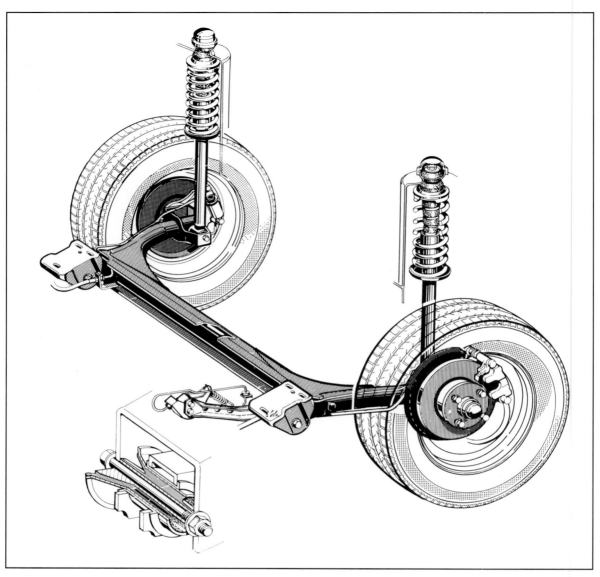

The torsion-beam rear suspension of the Golf is a neat piece of effective and simple design. This is the Mk2 version with internal anti-roll bar and disc brakes.

semi-flush side glass, the fixed quarter-lights being flush with the A-pillars. There was even an underbody deflector to direct airflow around the rear silencer.

An important point is that with the worldwide acceptance of the Golf, the new car had to reinforce VW's position in the class and perhaps also at the bottom of the next class up. With a more spacious engine bay, items like power steering and air conditioning were designed to be fitted if required, and proper RHD-configuration brake servo and wiper systems were part of the agenda this time around.

The basic mechanical layout emerged unscathed but a lot of work went into improving the engines and the running gear was revised. The engine and gearbox, suspension and steering were now carried on a rubber-mounted subframe. This also increased the torsional stiffness of the front end, improving the geometry of the front suspension in hard cornering. The engine and suspension were also rubber mounted and the total effect was to provide double insulation from road and mechanical noise. The subframe design also

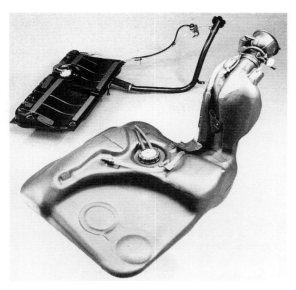

The new, moulded 12-gallon fuel tank, shaped to fit the available space in the rear axle area: behind it is the old 8.9-gallon tank.

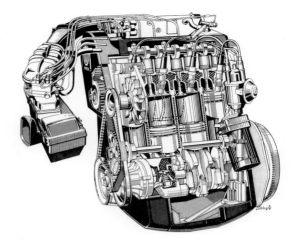

Cutaway of the GTI engine, in Mk2 form with water-cooled heat exchanger for the oil.

simplified assembly of the car, and the front part of the bodyshell was now bolted rather than welded in place. The basic concept of the cross-beam and trailing-arm rear suspension was retained but the beam was now moved aft to a position behind the pivot axis, about a third of the way along the arms to the wheels. This was done to reduce the camber change at the wheels under body roll. The section of the torsion beam was also changed from an inverted L-shape to a U on its side with the open end facing forwards. The anti-roll bar on the GTI version now ran inside that U-shaped section. The wheel travel of the new suspension was increased, offering a more comfortable ride. While standard Golfs still wore 13in diameter wheels, the GTI, with its four-wheel disc brake system, came with $6\frac{1}{2}$J x 14in steel wheels or Pirelli alloys with 185/60HR14 tyres as fitted to the Mk1 Campaign GTI. At last, the GTI had footwear that was up to the job.

Under the bonnet, there were quite a few changes. While the Bosch K-Jetronic injection had been retained, it was now arranged differently, with the metering unit mounted on the left rather than the right of the engine bay when looked at from the front. If anything, this made changing the now larger air filter an easier task. Further up the induction system, the twin-butterfly throttle body which had been 34/43mm on the Mk1 1.6

Comparison of the Mk1 (top) and Mk2 throttle bodies. Larger version helps to improve low-range torque and top-end power.

Underbonnet layout of an early Mk2 GTI shows the more spacious layout of the second-generation car. The most obvious change is the relocation of the fuel-injection air metering unit, bottom left in this picture.

and 38/45mm on the Mk1 1.8 was replaced by a 35/52mm unit, similar to that used on the 2.2-litre five-cylinder Audi cars. This enhanced low speed torque and also helped the engine breathe better at high revs. In combination with a new exhaust manifold and air-shrouded injectors, for better mixture control at low speeds, torque was boosted from 109lb/ft at 3,500rpm to 114lb/ft at 3,100rpm. Power remained the same at 112bhp but the engine speed at which it occurred dropped from 5,800rpm to 5,500rpm. Under the rocker cover, a new moulded plastic oil deflector (which can be fitted to older cars) ensured that oil splash fell back onto the camshaft where it was needed and was not thrown down the induction system. The oil cooler was now water cooled and the oil filter screwed into it.

The boot of the Golf 2 offered a 40% increase in capacity partly thanks to the adoption in most markets of a space-saver spare tyre. Fuel tank capacity was increased to a useful 12.1 gallons thanks to a new moulded tank nestled between the trailing arms. As with the Mk1 car, the new GTI was available in three or five-door format. But where the UK importer had only offered the three-door car in Britain before, the five-door was now also available. In North America, the GTI has always been three-door only.

The first round of cosmetic changes took place in 1985. With the launch of the 16-valve cars in the spring of that year, a new deep front spoiler became available. This had air intakes on either side that were ducted under the car to cool the larger vented front discs. Subsequent eight-valve cars had the same spoiler but with the intakes filled with a moulding. It is a simple matter to cut this out and fit the brake cooling ducts. Another obvious change was a revision of the exhaust system on the eight-valve car. The cut-out in the rear valance was widened and a twin-pipe silencer fitted. There was no power increase. The 16V cars were distinguished by their slightly lower ride height, distinctive alloy wheels and a rear roof-mounted aerial. This aerial had a built-in signal booster and had to be mounted aft to screen it from the high-output electronic ignition. 16V Sciroccos were equipped with the same feature.

The cars that journalists drove at the press launch had the optional power-assisted steering and luxury additions like electric window winders and electrically adjusted mirrors. Combined with good mechanical refinement, these extras made the Golf feel like a compact luxury car. Some drivers found the power steering too light and lacking in feedback, and indeed later GTIs with power steering have a heavier valve to give steering feel more in tune with the chassis responses.

The 16-valve engine
The eight-valve GTI engine in its two guises had long since proven its virtues. It had smoothness,

Second-generation Golf and Scirocco, here seen in 16V form, showing how much design trends had moved towards rounded forms since the more chisel-shaped originals. The rebodied Scirocco was still based on a Mk1-style floorpan.

The interior of the GTI 16V, with its leather-covered steering wheel, gear knob and gaiter and its new upholstery, had the air of a larger and more luxurious car, a feeling which was emphasized when power steering was included in the specification.

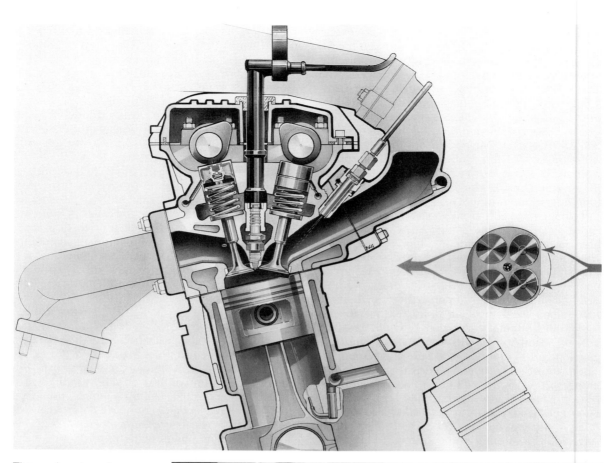

The exhaust valves are arranged perpendicularly in the 16V cylinder head, while the inlet valves are inclined at 25 degrees, a design which promotes better gas flow and is easier to produce than the more obvious symmetrical layout.

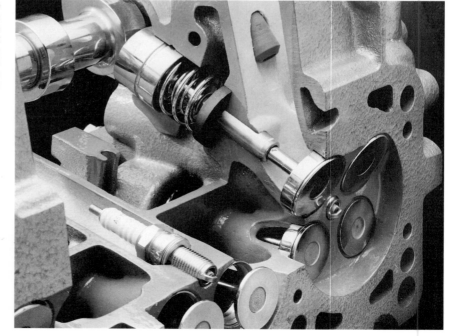

Close-up cutaway of the 16-valve head shows one of the compact hydraulic tappets between the cam and valve, and the central position of the sparking plug in the combustion chamber. The fuel-injection nozzle can be seen in the inlet tract above the valve.

In the 16-valve engine, the exhaust camshaft is belt-driven from the crankshaft and a roller chain at the other end of the head couples the two camshafts. The distributor is also driven directly from the exhaust camshaft instead of being mounted upright on the oil-pump drive as it is on the eight-valve unit.

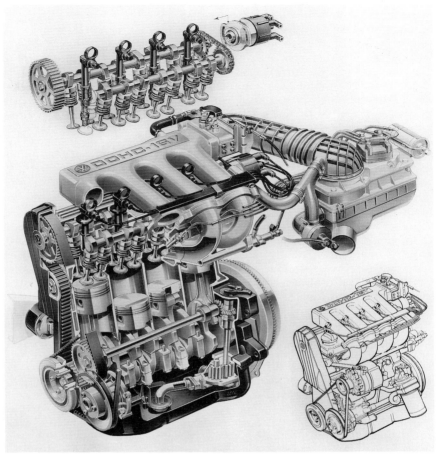

tractability and long-term reliability in its favour and seemed to be unburstable in long-distance high-speed running on German autobahns. But the competition had caught up with the GTI in terms of sheer power and the forthcoming Escort RS Turbo and Opel Kadett 2.0 GTE were definitely going to win the horsepower race.

VW looked at several possible ways to boost the GTI engine's output. The development department had experimented with turbocharging and found some very useful power increases by following that route. But turbo lag, dealer servicing difficulties, heat-soak problems and questionable long-term reliability were major potential snags, and VW's enviable reputation would be damaged if things went wrong out in the real world of customer use. Supercharging was tried as well, but the system as VW would have liked to see it was still in the experimental stage and would not reach a satisfactory level of development for mass production until 1988. The most sensible alternative to forced induction was

to go to four valves per cylinder, which in a four-cylinder engine like the GTI gives 16 valves, '16 ventiler' in German.

There are three main advantages of a four-valve-per-cylinder head: increased airflow with greater air velocity (even with smaller valves and lower lifts), lower valve train weight and hence inertia, and less valve lift required which equates to lower stress on the valve gear. The latter two factors help smooth and reliable running at high revs and minimize the power losses in the valve train. But the most important advantage from the engine output point of view is the first.

Ultimately, an engine is a device for burning an air-fuel mixture: how much power is produced is a function of how much of that mixture can be inducted, burnt and exhausted in a given time and how energy efficient in percentage terms the engine is. Compared with the traditional two-valve head, the four-valve layout provides better gas flow, and hence more efficient filling and emptying of the combustion chamber, both because a larger total valve area can be accommodated in a given engine and because the venturi effect of the smaller individual valves induces higher gas speeds. The part of the valve that makes the difference in gas flow is the circumference – the notional, annular path that the gas flows through as the valve lifts is known as the 'valve curtain'. In flowbench testing, it is immediately apparent that the pair of 34mm diameter inlet valves in the 16V GTI head flow substantially better than the single 40mm valve in the eight-valve head.

Before VW embarked on their own 16-valve head, two tuning firms had already produced such heads for the GTI. One was Graf in Austria and the other was the well known Oettinger company. Oettinger had traditionally had very close links with VW and there was some public co-operation between the two companies, VW using the Oettinger 16-valve head in the GTI 16S and in some experimental cars. So VW engineers already had experience of four-valve-per-cylinder engines. The development department concluded however that the complex Oettinger head with its large intake ports was too costly to make and lacked the torque and drivability they were looking for in a mass-production car. So VW began its own research and development programme which ended up taking five years.

During this period, and indeed into early production, the project was plagued by cracked heads, possibly due to exhaust-valve cooling problems. These early heads had a gear-driven exhaust camshaft like the Oettinger design and a different intake manifold configuration to the later production unit. The quieter roller-chain was eventually substituted for the gear drive, and when early production cars did not meet power and torque expectations, the intake manifold and camshafts were revised.

Most of these changes took place between the appearance of the 16V at the 1984 Frankfurt Show and the production cars being launched in 1985. The European-spec engine is referred to as type KR and has 139bhp at 6,100rpm with 124lb/ft at 4,600rpm. The version with catalytic convertor produces 129bhp at 6,000rpm and 124lb/ft at 4,250rpm. Both engines have a soft-cut rev limiter set at 7,200rpm. The non-cat version uses Bosch K-Jetronic fuel injection while the catalytic version has KE-Jetronic. Both have air-shrouded injectors, idle boost valve and over-run cut-off. The cat version has a knock sensor.

The 16V engine was made available in the GTI in America for the 1987 model year as part of the corporate image remake. The advent of electronic engine management controls has meant that US-spec engines now do not have the vast power discrepancies that once existed. The three-way catalyst equipped US-spec 16V engine was known as type PL and had 123bhp at 5,800rpm and 120lb/ft of torque at 4,250rpm, so it was not far behind the European catalytic cars. All 16V engines had a 10:1 CR. There was now no eight-valve GTI in the US, but the Golf GL and Jetta GL Carat cars in US spec now made a decent 105bhp at 5,400rpm and 107lb/ft of torque at 3,400rpm with Digifant fuel-injection. The older-style engine in the US Golf Cabriolet was rated at just 90bhp at 5,500rpm and 100lb/ft of torque at 3,000rpm.

There are two versions of the KR and PL engines. The A2 version is found in the Golf GTI, Jetta GTI and Corrado, while the A1 is peculiar to the Scirocco 16V. The distinction is made because the older, Mk1 floorpan of the Scirocco requires the mounting of the fuel metering unit on the opposite side of the engine bay. The intake manifolding is thus also different.

The chassis of the 16-valve cars was modified with 20% stiffer and slightly shorter springs and uprated dampers. Uprated front vented discs were fitted and 185/60VR14 tyres became standard. Alloy wheels were an option in Europe and standard in the UK and USA.

Looking further into the cylinder head, it is apparent that there are some clever design details. Unlike many other 16V designs, where the valves are angled symmetrically on each side of the head, the exhaust valves on the VW head actuate vertically along the bore centreline with the intake valves inclined at 25 degrees. This arrangement is conducive to better airflow and coincidentally makes the heads easier and therefore cheaper to manufacture. The exhaust valves are sodium-filled for improved cooling. That is an old idea that other manufacturers like Alfa Romeo were using back in the early 1970s but not with tiny 7mm diameter valve stems like in the VW. This is the fine art of German engineering in action! Another unusual feature is the location of the cam bearings between rather than on either side of the valves. This has the effect of reducing friction and thus wear, and the GTI 16V is the first production engine to use this idea. While the eight-valve engine and the Oettinger 16-valve unit had solid bucket tappets, with shim adjustment for valve clearances, the VW 16V head has self-adjusting

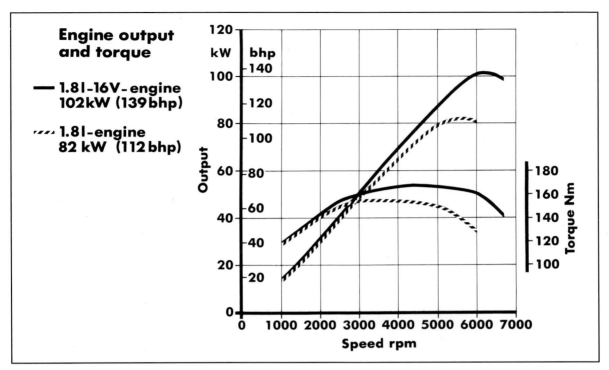

Engine output and torque

— **1.8l-16V-engine 102kW (139bhp)**

⁄⁄⁄ **1.8l-engine 82 kW (112bhp)**

Graph comparing power and torque curves of the 1.8-litre eight and 16-valve engines. It emphasizes that the four-valves-per-cylinder unit is both more powerful and torquier than the earlier design.

The American-market version of the Mk2 GTI was distinguished by rectangular headlamps and also had different bumpers and a different style of alloy wheel from its European counterpart. This is a 1985 model.

31

hydraulic tappets for quieter running and long-term durability. Once regarded as unsuitable for high-revving engines and decried by the enthusiast, hydraulic tappets (lifters in American parlance) have been much developed, and were sanctified for use in performance cars by their inclusion in the engine of the Porsche 928.

Driving conditions in the US are somewhat different from Europe. In Germany, you can drive flat-out on the autobahns and in most countries the speed limit is at least 70mph. With 55mph or 65mph being the limit in different parts of the US, the emphasis is on low-end and mid-range torque. The exhaust camshaft is the same on US and Euro versions of the 16V, but on the intake side, the US cam is ground for 0.025in less lift and 12 degrees less duration. The US cam thus has 0.353in lift compared to 0.378in on the Euro version. Taking 0.050in of lift as a common measure, the US cam gives 196 degrees duration compared to 208 degrees for the Euro cam. These changes enhance the low-speed torque for the different driving conditions.

While the 16V head sits on a similar 1,781cc block to the eight-valver, an important internal difference is the incorporation of oil squirters to direct cooling oil at the underside of the pistons, reflecting the expectation of hard flat-out autobahn driving. Both eight and 16V motors have forged crankshafts. 16V pistons are flat-topped with a chamfered edge and valve relief cut into the top surface. The skirts are shorter than those of the eight-valver and have thicker-walled wrist pins for high-rpm durability.

Hydraulic tappets were introduced to the eight-valve engine in 1986. In 1987 there was a minor facelift with the door mirrors being moved forward and the quarter lights deleted, a new steering wheel, and thicker bump protection strips on the sides of the car. Different alloy wheels with teardrop-shape cutouts were used on UK eight-valve cars and the seat fabric was changed. In 1988, a digital instrument panel was offered as an option on the 16V in Europe.

For the 1990/91 model year, the US-spec Golfs were further uprated. The eight-valve car, now quoted as having 105bhp at 5,400rpm and 110lb/ft at 3,400rpm (100bhp and 100lb/ft in California) got many of the goodies found previously on the now defunct 1.8-litre 16V. These included the teardrop-style 6J x 14in alloy wheels, 16V-spec suspension and power steering.

1987 model three-door eight-valve GTI showing new wheels, revised side glass and door mirrors, and thicker bump protection moulding.

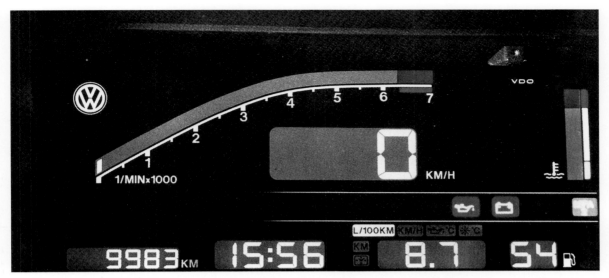

Trendy technology: this VDO-made digital instrument pack was offered as an option on 1988 model-year GTI 16V cars, aping the Audi quattro. It was not popular.

The second gear ratio was changed to 1.94:1 (from 2.12:1) for better acceleration.

But the big news was the adoption of the 2-litre (1,984cc) Passat block for the 16-valve model. With 134bhp at 5,800rpm and 133lb/ft of torque at 4,400rpm, this engine, equipped with a catalytic convertor, at last gave the GTI European levels of performance. The Golf shared the engine and 6J x 15in BBS wheels with the Jetta GLi 16V, turning them into a pair of the hottest compact cars you could buy in the States. Now that the USA and South Africa have moved over to a 2-litre version of the 16V engine, it is surely only a matter of time before all GTIs in other markets do the same to redress the power losses caused by ever-tightening emission laws.

The G60 supercharger

The Corrado G60 and Rallye Golf were first seen by the public in the autumn of 1988, but the supercharger development programme dates back as far as 1973, a year before the first Scirocco was launched.

Experiments then were conducted on the air-cooled flat-four Beetle engine using both turbo-charging and supercharging. When the water-cooled engine for the Golf went into production, further effort initially concentrated on turbo-charging. VW engineering policy, however, dictated that certain goals such as longevity and tractability were more important than sheer horsepower, and the line of development switched to mechanically driven superchargers. Turbo-

charging technology had come from diesel engines used on commercial vehicles and indeed the diesel, with its good low-end torque endowed by high compression ratios, suited turbocharging better than small-capacity petrol engines. Today, VW use a turbo to good effect in the Golf Turbo Diesel.

VW chose supercharging in preference to the currently more fashionable turbocharging. This cutaway of the G-lader unit shows the spiral in the housing and the centre bearing.

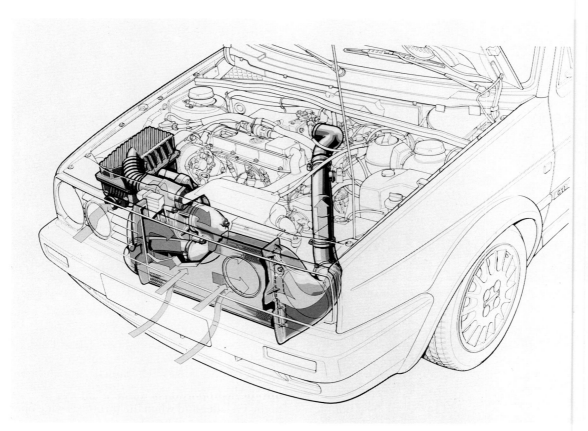

Intercooler system of the GTI G60. Air enters the filter then passes through the fuel-injection metering unit, the G-lader, the intercooler across the front of the car and into the inlet manifold on the back of the engine.

At the time, the only available supercharger units were American and a Magnussen, a Roots-type blower, was tried. This proved difficult to pair with the intercooler that VW saw as necessary for high-performance applications. Then the engineers came across an old idea that had not worked before because of lack of the necessary machine precision and suitable alloys when it was invented – in 1905! Patented by a Frenchman by the name of L. Creux 70 years before VW engineers decided to pursue it, the G-lader or G-shaped supercharger is similar to a Wankel rotary engine in principle, but uses the eccentric rotation of a displacer within a double spiral to compress the air.

Early results seemed discouraging. But VW's test standards are exacting. A current production G-lader must be able to withstand running at full output for 800 hours at a continuous 10,000rpm. That is very harsh treatment when you consider that an early unit that failed after just four hours on the dyno lasted 20,000 test miles in a car.

With the design problems sorted out, pro-ductionizing the G-lader was the next hurdle. The specifications of the design are such that very precise tolerances must be adhered to. The thin alloy walls of the G-charger have to be machined to a precision of 0.5mm and to achieve this, VW tooling engineers had to develop a new computer-controlled high-speed milling process. Despite this, the actual production output of the units is still dependent on the skilled workers who undertake final assembly of the precision components.

Proceeding with the same caution shown when they released the lower-volume Scirocco ahead of the Golf, VW let out a small-production special edition of the Polo 1.3 with the G-lader. Designations for VW's G-lader cars go according to the depth of the working chambers on each side of the supercharger. Thus, the Polo was dubbed the G40 and all the 1.8-litre cars are G60s. The small Polo G40 produced 110bhp, making it as powerful as the original GTI. In a lighter, more slippery car, this sort of power gave it quite spectacular performance. With several years of reliable running under its belt, the G-lader Polo is a proven formula.

Although the G-lader places less thermal stress on an engine than a turbo, internal work still had to be done to ensure engine longevity. The familiar eight-valve 1,781cc engine with hydraulic tappets, Digifant fuel-injection, catalytic convertor and knock sensor is the base. The intake valves have current spec VW hardened coating but the cylinder head is heat-treated to withstand the thermal stresses of a higher output. The exhaust valves are sodium-filled like the 16V's. The pistons are cast rather than forged but have thicker wrist pins and the compression ratio has been dropped to 8:1. The Digifant engine management system looks after ignition and fuelling as in the normal eight-valve car but in the G60 it is also assigned the task of boost control. The knock sensor works to allow the car to operate at lower boost pressures if fuel quality drops. At the onset of detonation, the ignition advance is reduced and beyond that, boost pressure is released through a computer-controlled valve built into the idle stabilizer system.

The blower is driven in two parts by a double belt system. The external poly-vee belt drives the blower at 1.6 times engine speed. Inside the unit is a drive and secondary shaft that 'wobble' a displacer in the working chambers. The second, smaller belt spins the lightweight magnesium displacer precisely to give the unit its timing. Air enters the air filter and passes through the air metering box of the fuel-injection system and into the G-lader's intake. The air enters a wedge-shaped working chamber and is pushed around the spiral of the housing and out at the other end. No compression has taken place yet. The charge air now heads for the intercooler which is the key to the whole installation. Whenever air is forced to travel like this, it gets hot and this reduces its density and the engine's potential power. Another problem is that it can cause pre-ignition. The intercooler drops the charge air temperature by as much as 130 degrees F, helping to increase engine power and delay the onset of detonation. The air, now cooled, makes its way up to the throttle body. This is different from the one used on naturally aspirated GTI engines and has a bypass valve to enhance fuel economy at part throttle and when cruising. This is linked directly to the throttle linkage and operates in reverse. When the throttle is closed, the bypass is fully open, cycling the compressed air back to the G-lader. At part throttle, a proportion of the air is allowed to return to the G-lader and when the throttle is wide open, the engine gets full boost.

The VW G-lader is an efficient device

Cutaway of the complete G60 power unit showing the internal components of the engine and the belt-driven G-lader unit.

Neat underbonnet installation of the GTI G60, an engine bay packed tight with technology. Of note is the absence of the heat shielding needed with turbocharged systems.

compared to conventional superchargers. A traditional Roots-type blower has an efficiency of about 40%. The G-lader offers 65% and requires about 2bhp to spin when the car is doing 40mph. On maximum boost, the unit requires 17.4bhp. This equates to a maximum output of 175bhp minus the driving power for the blower. The G60 cars are thus rated at 160bhp at the flywheel, at 5,800rpm, with 166lb/ft of torque at 3,800rpm.

The intercooler in the Corrado G60 is situated on the left-hand side of the car due to aero-dynamic and styling demands. Although it is rated at the same power as the Rallye Golf, the latter, with its competition orientation, is homologated with a larger, full-width intercooler across the front of the radiator. In terms of engine response, 80% of maximum charge pressure is achieved 0.4 seconds after the throttle is depressed fully and

full boost follows 0.4 seconds after that.

The Rallye Golf

As this is being written, the Rallye Golf programme is going through some turmoil. It is not VW's fault and no reflection on the car. It is the fickle-minded officialdom of FISA, the international motorsport body, that is once again causing trouble. In 1989, they imposed a 40mm restrictor on the G60 engine which would have limited power output to about 230bhp compared to the near 300bhp level that turbocharged engines can achieve. On appeal, FISA gave VW a year to run without the restrictor, but the long-term future of VW's newest rally weapon is uncertain. It is precisely for homologation for rallysport that the 5,000 LHD-only Rallye Golfs were to be made at VW's Belgian plant in Brussels for sale to customers in certain markets. With VW Motorsport driver Erwin Weber at the wheel, the 4WD syncro Rallye Golf was run in the Sachs Winter Rally as the course car. Unofficially, it was fastest on 15 of the 22 special stages! More testing was done in Sardinia in April 1990 for the Costa Smeralda Rally with a redesigned, strengthened transmission. The car made its Group A debut in the Acropolis Rally but was unlucky to be forced out early on with suspension damage. On the New Zealand Rally, regular driver Weber scored a very creditable third overall behind Toyota and Mazda, teams with much more rallying development experience to draw on. Even if the car is not eligible for 1991, some successful results in its first year will have proved a point for VW.

In line with its role as a homologation car, the Rallye Golf has flared wheelarches to accommodate wider wheels and tyres, and one-piece front and rear panels with integrated spoilers. Brakes are ventilated discs all round. Rectangular homofocal broad-beam headlamps are used. The car sits 20mm lower than the Golf syncro whose 4WD system it shares. The springs, dampers and anti-roll bars are uprated from the GTI 16V specification. The syncro system splits the torque between front and rear according to conditions. On dry roads, most of the power goes through the front wheels. The moment the front wheels start to lose traction on a slippery surface or during hard acceleration, more power is fed to the rear wheels by the viscous coupling, spreading the driving load and compensating for rearward weight transfer.

Although the engine is nominally identical in output to that used in the G60-equipped Golf and Corrado, its capacity has been reduced from 1,781cc to 1,763cc to avoid moving up a class in motorsport classification because of the multiplication factor applied to forced-aspiration engines. The gearbox is the 02A unit first seen in the new Passat: this is its first application both in a Golf and with four-wheel drive. It is lighter and more compact than earlier boxes, but also stronger to take the power of the supercharged engine. A little-known fact is that this gearbox was originally developed in France, and first used in competition in South Africa where VWSA rallied a 2-litre 16-valve version of the Golf syncro. The French box was initially not up to the task, so it was redesigned in South Africa by Andre Verwey, one of the world leaders in competition gearbox

The huge wheelarch flares of the Rallye Golf leave room for much larger wheels and tyres. Only 5,000 cars were built, the number required for motorsport homologation.

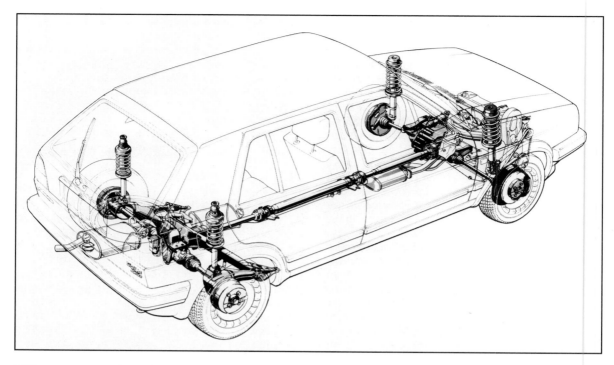

VW's syncro system is used on the Rallye Golf and the G60 Limited (as well as some lower-powered models): it feeds power to the rear wheels through a viscous coupling when the front wheels begin to run out of traction.

design. Its subsequent performance in the factory Group A car proved its new-found strength.

In standard road trim, the Golf Rallye has a 130mph top speed and a 7.6-second 0-60mph capability. To achieve motorsport homologation in Group A for 1990, 5,000 cars had to be built by September 1989. But the demand for the car from customers wanting the ultimate Golf pushed VW to think seriously about building a further 5,000 in 1990. Scheduled to appear in late 1990 is a Golf GTI G60 syncro which will be a volume-production version of the Rallye lacking the large wheelarches and with its engine capacity restored to 1,781cc.

Golf Country

At the 1989 Geneva Show, VW exhibited a Golf for serious off-road use. Dubbed the Montana, the vehicle was developed to explore the market potential for a comfortable passenger car with proper off-road capabilities. Unlike other 4WD road cars, the Montana had sufficient ground clearance (half as much again as a standard syncro) for off-road use and a 25-degree approach angle. Engineers raided the VW parts bin to make this car which was powered by the 1.8-litre 98bhp fuel-injected engine. A

framework of spacers between the body and axles, with new suspension struts and dampers, raised the car. Front and rear nudge bars, auxiliary lights with wire mesh stoneguards and a sturdy sump protection plate added the finishing touches. On subsequent appearances, the vehicle had its name changed from Montana to Country. In response to customer demand, it looked set to become a production reality in 1990.

Golf G60

For the 1990 model year, a major facelift for the Golf and Jetta range was undertaken. The bumpers were visually integrated with the body-work, with new front and rear valances, the front one carrying a neat bib spoiler. The black plastic wheelarch extensions were now joined by neat side sills. The 16V and G60 Golfs got foglamps built into the front spoiler and UK 16V cars came with 6J x 15 BBS 'classic' alloy wheels shod with 185/55VR15 tyres. There were no plans to offer a right-hand-drive G60 in the near future. In Continental European markets there was a 6½J x 15 BBS split-rim wheel option with 195/50VR15 tyres, also offered for the Corrado G60. For the Continent again there was an 'Edition One' package for all GTIs and this included the split-

Initially called the Montana but later retitled Country, VW's prototype for a cross-country Golf first appeared at the 1989 Geneva Show. A fuel-injection engine and four-wheel-drive were combined with radically revised suspension mountings to give the vehicle a genuine off-road capability.

Most highly developed volume-production version of the Golf is the GTI G60, capable of 135mph straight out of the box – almost the ultimate hot hatchback.

rim BBS wheels, Recaro seats and special paint-work in metallic quartz, metallic black or dark burgundy. The rear lights were partially darkened, the front indicators were white (when unlit), and the side and rear window glass had been given a chrome treatment. Finishing touches were a leather-covered steering wheel and gear-lever knob. VW were clearly learning from the aftermarket industry!

At the 1990 Geneva Show, the Golf GTI G60 was announced. This addition to the high-performance Golf line-up meant that there were now three GTI variants as well as the homologation special Rallye. Most of the technology had been seen already on the Corrado G60, including the ABS and the uprated brakes that can only be used with 15in wheels. An innovation was the EDL (Electronic Differential Lock), available as an option. This used the ABS sensors to assist in extracting the last drop of traction from a powerful front-wheel-drive car. Unlike a mechanical diff lock, the EDL, it is claimed, does not affect the steering.

Compared to a standard eight-valve GTI, the 16V had a ride height 10mm lower all round. The G60 was a further 10mm lower at the front and had thicker anti-roll bars – 23mm front and 21mm rear, compared with 20mm and 18mm for the other two GTIs. Low-friction Passat-style dampers were specified for a good ride. The transmission was the MQ unit from the Passat and Corrado and the gearbox and final drive ratios were different from other GTIs.

In the latest round of legislative changes in Europe, with tightening emission controls coming into force as 1992 approaches, Britain and Italy are the only two countries still getting the 112bhp GTI and 139bhp GTI 16V. In Germany, the new cars all have catalytic convertors. The current-spec GTI has 107bhp at 5,400rpm and 115lb/ft of torque at 3,800rpm, while the 16V is still the same as the cat version launched in 1985 with 129bhp at 5,800bhp and 124lb/ft at 4,250rpm.

The G60 specification – 160bhp and 135mph – is a long way from the first GTI's 110bhp and 110mph. The engineers who took it upon themselves to work out of hours on a 'Sport Golf' back in 1974 must be proud to see their child come of age. In 1990, the GTI is sweet sixteen.

Booted companion

With a three-door and a five-door hatchback as well as a sporty coupe in their catalogue of new cars, VW were doing very well in the small-car market in the mid to late 1970s. But there was also a growing segment of the motoring public who felt that a hatchback was utilitarian and lacked the formality required for business use or to suit a mature driver. Not to miss a marketing opportunity, VW set about adding a boot to the Golf, and in late 1979 announced the Jetta. An apparent reference to the Jet Stream in line with VW's fad for naming cars after winds, the Jetta was aimed at buyers who wanted the performance, nimble handling and fuel efficiency of the Golf in a more formal package.

VW stylists took the wedge-shaped frontal treatment of the Golf and applied it to the rear of the car, giving it a nicely balanced look. In doing so, they added 15 inches to the overall length of the car on the Golf's 94.5in wheelbase. This made the Jetta into a considerably larger car which was in the BMW 3-Series size class. As a saloon requires less structural stiffening than a hatchback, the weight increase was just 65lb. The 17.5cu ft boot was huge for a car of its size, as capacious as the Audi 100's, and the car was a genuine long-distance tourer for four people and their luggage.

Engine options were the same as for the Golf, and of course there was the 110bhp fuel-injected Jetta GLi which, like the rest of the range, was available in two or four-door form. In Britain, only the four-door GLi was sold, and in this market, alloy wheels were standard. The Golf was the more popular car in Britain, but different buyer attitudes elsewhere sometimes reversed that situation. In Singapore for instance, the greater

GTI brio in a formal suit: the Jetta GLi was a discreet high-performance saloon that must have caused some red faces amongst the boy-racer brigade.

The Jetta was also offered in two-door form on the Continent where the configuration is more popular than in Britain.

The Jetta Mk2 managed to look more like a design in its own right rather than a modified Golf. This is a two-door 112bhp GT version.

social acceptability of a three-box saloon meant that the Jetta GLi outsold the Golf GTI three-to-one. But the buyer profile was totally different. GTI buyers wanted to buy the GTI; Jetta customers were looking for a sporty small saloon with the VW reputation for reliability and good quality. But sales of the GLi version were not spectacular, so when the 1.6-litre GTI engine was terminated in summer 1982 in favour of the 1.8-litre unit, the Jetta GLi was deleted. The most powerful version then, until the advent of the Jetta Mk2 GT, was a 1,588cc 85bhp carburettor car with the 4+E gearbox.

The Jetta Mk2 was designed into the new Golf

Interior of a Jetta GLX (above) with cabin furniture practically identical to the Golf's. The 1987 GTX 16V (below), with distinctive front and rear spoilers and alloy wheels, was an accomplished sports saloon to rival the BMW 320i.

Jetta GT 16V for the 1990 model-year, showing the new-style bumpers and 6J x 15in BBS alloy wheels.

programme from day one rather than as an after-thought like the original. Like its progenitor, the new Jetta used rectangular headlamps to distinguish it from its Golf brother although US-spec Golf Mk2s use these lights as well. Where the Mk1 Golf and Jetta had drag coefficients of 0.42 and 0.43 respectively, the revised cars manage 0.34 and 0.36. Jetta Mk2 had a 21cu ft boot, as big as a Volvo 760's and bigger than the old BMW 5-Series.

In Germany there was a luxury version known as the Jetta Carat in 1985, which some compared to the Mercedes-Benz 190. The Carat had the 90bhp 1.8-litre carburettor engine and in passenger space offered more legroom than the Mercedes and indeed the BMW 3-Series. Its boot was much larger than either of its rivals and the VW gave away little in build quality either. The Jetta Carat is a current luxury model in the USA. The high performance Jetta in 1984-6 was the 112bhp GT with the engine from the GTI. When the 16-valve engine was dropped into the Jetta, the tame-looking VW saloon became a real wolf in sheep's clothing with performance very close to its hatchback brother. In terms of hand-ling, some drivers prefer the Jetta because it turns in better: with the weight of the extra sheetmetal, the greater rearward mass distribution helps to neutralize understeer in corners.

In 1985, the US market got the Jetta GLi with a 100bhp 1.8-litre engine fuelled with the Bosch KE-Jetronic injection system. This went down very well and established the Jetta as a sporty, quality saloon in the compact imported car market. By 1987, the 16V engine had found its way to the US in the GTI and the GLi 16V was launched. Every year, VW of America commission their Wolfsburg Limited-Edition cars. The 1989 Wolfsburg Limited-Edition Jetta GLi 16V had special paintwork, BBS 6J x 15in alloy wheels, central locking, electric windows, Recaro seats, sunroof, air conditioning and a good stereo system along with the 123bhp 16V engine. A very attractive package indeed.

After using the GTX designation in Europe in 1987, VW have returned to the GT suffix for the sporty models. Thus in the face-lifted 1990 models, the GT has the eight-valve 107bhp engine and the GT 16V has the 129bhp power unit.

2

Blowing hot: Scirocco

'Scirocco' is the German and Italian spelling of Sirocco, a hot, dry African wind that blows across the Mediterranean to Italy, Sicily and Spain. It was the name Wolfsburg chose for the sleek, neatly chiselled Italianate coupe that would share its floorpan, engine and suspension with the car that would make or break VW's fortunes, the Golf. The whole project was a bold one. Giugiaro's studio, Ital Design, were commissioned to clothe the two cars, saloon and coupe, and both the new range of engines and the revolutionary torsion-beam rear axle were something of a tour de force in that market sector at the time. The unquestionable success of the Golf and Scirocco has become legendary. But in 1974 VW were still smarting from the lack of sales success of the K70 in a market slot that is today well served by the Jetta. Anxious not to perpetate another disaster, which might have finished the company, they slipped the low-volume Karmann-produced Scirocco onto the market first, ahead of the Golf, to test the water and prove the service reliability of the new underpinnings.

Some onlookers were puzzled, expecting a Beetle successor, to see first what was more a replacement for the Beetle-based Karmann Ghia than for the Beetle itself. But the inversion of the historical precedent, whereby a coupe is almost always launched after the saloon, paid off handsomely. The Golf went on to beat even the Beetle's sales success, and it spawned the GTI which, 16 years on, is still the car that all pretenders to the hot-hatchback crown must measure up to. The Scirocco, latterly in 16-valve form, held its position as the fastest VW right up until, eight years into its second incarnation, it was

at last usurped by the Corrado.

The famous Italian stylist Giorgetto Giugiaro has an evident liking for wedge shapes, and it is therefore no surprise that the Alfasud Sprint, released two years after the Scirocco, bears more than a passing resemblance to the German car. As all manufacturers tend to do when they 'productionize' a car, VW claim to have cleaned up the Giugiaro design. Fortunately, they did little to alter the car's overall look, and what we ended up with was a simple and aesthetically pleasing compact coupe with a 94.5in wheelbase and an overall length of 12ft 7.5in. Visibility was good through the large glass area which was a distinctive feature of the design, but rear-seat leg and headroom were not strong points. Even the larger Scirocco Mk2 is noted as being a 2+2 rather than a four-seater.

The Scirocco Mk1 made its debut with a choice of three engines; a 50bhp 1,093cc unit from the little hatchback Audi 50 which later became the VW Polo, and two 1,471cc engines, one with 70bhp and the other with 85bhp. All had single overhead camshafts, toothed-belt driven, and were water cooled. The engine was placed transversely across the nose of the car over the front wheels and with an in-line gearbox arrangement. The larger capacity units were canted 20 degrees backwards and the smaller engine 15 degrees forwards to achieve the same mass distribution in all cases. The specific orientation which placed the gearbox on the left of the car in this non-crossflow engine design made the exhaust installation simpler and gave plenty of room for the brake servo in left-hand-drive models although, as we will see later, this created a problem in right-

This early Scirocco shows the rectangular headlamp style that differentiated the domestic base models from the more upmarket four-headlamp cars which were the ones that were exported.

hand-drive cars. An integral final drive unit behind the gearbox was responsible for passing power to a pair of unequal length tubular drive shafts (unequal in diameter also, to equalize torque effects) with constant velocity joints at each end. Coil-sprung MacPherson struts and an anti-roll bar made up the front suspension, while the rear suspension consisted of VW's novel torsion beam system with its trailing arms in conjunction with coil springs and tubular dampers. The later GLi model got uprated suspension and a rear anti-roll bar.

In its 85bhp form, the Scirocco was a respectable performer with a top speed of 106mph and a 0-60mph time of 10.7 seconds, but it did not begin to show its true potential, like the Golf, until the 110bhp fuel-injected engine was dropped into it in late 1976. Maximum speed went up to 115mph and the 0-60mph sprint now only took 8.8 seconds, quite enough to blow away unsuspecting sports cars or big saloons of 2 litres or more that might have had a go at the traffic lights. And this was with a four-speed gearbox!

The early Scirocco TS had garishly checked fabric upholstery inset into vinyl seats. The fuel-injected GLi version adopted much more subdued and higher-quality plain coloured fabric, and in 1978, when the car received a facelift with new, longer plastic-faced bumpers and redesigned front and rear side lamp clusters, the interior was also revised. The tombstone high-backed seats were replaced with seats with separate headrests and the spindly sports steering wheel with its three drilled spokes was replaced with a more substantial three-spoke unit which the GLS and GLi Sciroccos then shared with the Golf GTI. In those days, the Scirocco also shared its instrument panel with the Golf GTI except that the facia was silver and the GTI's was black.

The Americans were over the moon with the swift little Scirocco. Emissions and safety had been big issues in the States since the late 1960s, and the first Sciroccos to reach America in 1975 were thus equipped with catalytic convertors. Power loss through emission controls meant that only the larger engine was sent across the Atlantic,

46

The seats in VW's new Scirocco must have left clowns without their trousers all over Germany.

and in US trim, the 1,471cc engine was reduced to 70bhp at 6,000rpm with torque of 81lb/ft at 3,500rpm. This was still enough to give a top speed of 103mph and the car took 12.7sec to reach 60mph. Amongst the emasculated, bigger-engined American cars, this was still quick. The factory addressed the 5mph bumper regulations by using the Euro bumpers and mounting them on hydraulic impact absorbing tubes. This increased the length of the car by 3.5in. Only one model was offered, simply known as the Volkswagen Scirocco.

In Germany, the trim choice for the cars depended on the GL (luxury) or GT (sporting) designation, and early fuel-injected cars brought into the UK were of GLi spec. In 1980, VAG (UK) Ltd decided that the faster Scirocco should share some of the cachet attaching to the Golf GTI and be further differentiated from its carburettored GLS sister. Thus, the last model year of the Scirocco Mk1 in Britain found the car being sold with a GTi badge, GTI-type sports seats with sporting patterned cloth trim, digital idling stabilization for its engine and the new five-speed gearbox also introduced in the Golf.

While the Scirocco was launched with a 1,471cc engine of 76.5mm x 80.0mm bore and stroke giving 85bhp at 5,800rpm and 89lb/ft of

torque at 3,200rpm on a 9.7:1 compression ratio, it soon became obvious that advancing emission regulations and the wish to improve drivability required some minor changes to the engine specification. For the 1976 model year, the engine's bore was increased to 79.5mm thus making the power unit practically square. Power remained at 85bhp but this was now developed 200rpm lower and torque increased by 3lb/ft but 600rpm further up the scale. Significantly, the compression ratio was dropped to 8.2:1 which allowed the engine to use two-star fuel. It was this 1,588cc engine that formed the basis of the GTI power unit. With a different cylinder head that was effectively flat with the combustion chambers in the piston tops in the so-called Heron design, this engine produced 110bhp at 6,100rpm and 101lb/ft of torque at 5,000rpm, fed by Bosch K-Jetronic fuel-injection. Compression ratio was 9.7:1, requiring four-star fuel.

The 1,588cc engine was introduced to the United States in 1976 and at the same time, front seat height adjusters were added and the two windscreen wipers replaced with a single one as in Europe. Big news for the 1977 model year though was the adoption of the Bosch K-Jetronic fuel-injection used in the Euro GTi/GLi models to help recoup some of the power and drivability lost

Neat tail-end styling of the Giugiaro-designed Scirocco, here in the facelifted version with neater wraparound bumpers.
This GLi has the alloy wheels also used on the Golf GTI.

through US emission controls. The more precise fuel metering of the injection system was an aid in itself towards meeting the clean air regulations. The 1977 car was called the Super Scirocco and actually had only 76bhp at 5,500rpm but 87lb/ft of torque at 3,200rpm. While that sounds very weak-kneed by European standards, it is torque rather than bhp that gives acceleration and good drivability, and these were still adequate to give the Super Scirocco a 105mph top speed and a 10.5sec 0-60mph capability. This performance compares very favourably with the European 85bhp GLS version.

And then in 1978, increasingly strict emission controls caused VW to take what on the surface appeared to be a retrograde step. The engine's stroke was shortened to 73.4mm from 80mm, thereby reducing displacement from 1,588cc to 1,457cc, 14cc less than the original small bore 1,471cc engine. Power dropped from 76bhp at 5,500rpm to just 71bhp at 5,800rpm and torque was knocked back 10lb/ft to 73lb/ft at 3,500rpm. These were the figures for the 49-State version. Tighter legislation in California where the smog problem was worse saw Sciroccos with 1bhp and

1lb/ft of torque less than even those figures. Other modifications included new plastic-covered 5mph impact bumpers rather like the European versions, but visibly longer and with a chrome centre decoration strip. A larger front spoiler, like that on the Euro GLi, was fitted along with a larger radiator, bigger brake servo, additional sound insulation, a wood-grain instrument panel and a remote-control door mirror. Ironically perhaps, the 1978 Scirocco was no slower on the 0-60mph sprint, still taking 10.4 seconds to cover this measure. It was slower over the standing quarter-mile though. Top speed dropped to 104mph, which was hardly significant, but fuel consumption actually benefited very slightly.

The smaller engine only lasted a year. 1979 saw the 1,588cc engine reinstated, but with 78bhp at 5,500rpm and 84lb/ft at 3,200rpm. California cars had 2bhp and 1lb/ft less. All this chopping and changing gives you some idea how much trouble the ever tightening US emission legislation was causing the motor industry as a whole at that time. Manufacturers were still experimenting with all sorts of permutations to meet emission

48

In the USA, a car externally similar to the Storm was sold as the Scirocco 'S', but it lacked both the leather interior trim and the GTI engine.

The smart Scirocco Storm, with a front spoiler in body colour and a leather-trimmed interior, was a UK-only model.

levels and yet keep performance, drivability and economy all at reasonable levels. It was a juggling act that some performed better than others and VW still managed to turn out a product that gained high praise from US magazine testers and customers. A far cry indeed from the brickbats deservedly thrown at home-grown automobiles of the era, one or two of which this writer had the misfortune to drive.

To coincide with the facelift, VW introduced the five-speed gearbox in the 1979 model year as well. This was standard on Euro GTi/GLi cars but an optional extra in America. In the US version, VW kept the original four-speed ratios, including the 0.97:1 overdrive fourth, and added a 0.76:1 fifth gear. To balance things out, they changed the final-drive ratio, going from 3.90:1 to 4.17:1. The intention was to improve both acceleration and fuel economy. The front angled bib spoiler was replaced with a Kamei-made vertical air dam which gave the car a lower, more purposeful look and this was carried over to the more heavily specified Scirocco S versions available in the next two model years as a limited edition in Cirrus Grey metallic, Cosmos Silver and Mars Red in addition to black and white. Sports seats were from the Euro Golf GTI. Throughout all this, the US versions of the Scirocco Mk1 were fitted with the same slightly convex 5J x 13in alloy wheels with 175/70SR13 tyres that adorned the European GLS. Only the 110bhp Euro-spec cars wore 5½J x 13in alloy wheels, of similar pattern, shod with 175/70HR13 rubber.

The Scirocco S bore the Kamei front spoiler in the US market, and a limited-edition model in the UK used the same part. Commissioned by VAG (UK) Ltd, this very upmarket Scirocco, dubbed the Scirocco Storm, was aimed at potential buyers of the six-cylinder BMW 3-Series cars. With its leather trim, colour-coded front spoiler and distinctive paintwork, this attractive luxury coupe sold out like hot cakes. It was offered in 1979 and 1980 in its first guise with the two available colours being Diamond Silver Green metallic with black hide leather and Black metallic with fawn hide leather. For the 1981 model year, the last production year of the Scirocco Mk1, the Storm arrived in its definitive version with two new colours, Diamond Silver Blue metallic with blue hide leather or Brown metallic with tan hide leather. Distinctive multi-spoke alloy wheels from the VW Passat character-ized this penultimate Scirocco Mk1 and these cars are the most collectable of the old shape Sciroccos. Good examples command more money than early Scirocco GTi Mk2s.

Scirocco 2

As it was released first, the Scirocco was due for replacement before the Golf. Good as it was dynamically even at the end of its tenure, it was packaging and aerodynamics that held it at a disadvantage against newer rivals. Thus for the 1982 model year, a new Scirocco was born. Scirocco 2 was publicly unveiled at the 1981 Geneva Show and instantly provoked strong reactions from the press. Many journalists thought the car bore some resemblance to the show car Giugiaro had introduced at the 1976 Turin Show. The BMW-based Asso di Quadri (Ace of Diamonds) was indeed superficially similar to the new VW in proportions, and especially in its roof treatment. But it was a more

The Scirocco Mk2 was the new coupe for 1982, with in-house styling by VW's own design department this time. This is an American-spec car with side-protection moulding and ungainly 5mph impact bumpers.

The interior trim of the 1981 1.6-litre Scirocco Mk2 GTI (right) was distinguished by a bold rectangular pattern. This was replaced by a more subtle check-pattern cloth (below) with the advent of the 1.8-litre car in late 1982.

angular car in both profile and section; it belonged to a generation of design ideas that was slowly being eroded by more rounded, aerodynamic styles of which the new Scirocco was one example.

Why then, came the next question, was the new VW coupe not designed by Giugiaro who had after all penned the shapes of the three cars (Golf, Scirocco and Passat) that had pulled the Wolfsburg firm back from the brink of disaster? The answer to that is that Giugiaro had submitted two of the five proposals that went before the PSK (Product Strategie Kommission). Other designers, including the famous and highly individualistic German stylist Luigi Colani, had submitted proposals but the five shortlisted were the two Giugiaro designs and three done in-house by Herbert Schafer, Director of VW Design. In such decisions, adherence to the democratic process ensures that the committee do not know who is responsible for each design; all the mock-ups are painted the same colour and finished to the same standard.

The winner was the one that best satisfied the company's brief in terms of improved aerodynamics with reduced lift, best use of interior space for both passengers and luggage, and attractive styling. The designers had been given the constraints of the existing Scirocco platform within which to work but told that the overall bodyshell dimensions were expected to increase. Extra weight and material costs were also expected as larger dimensions would mean more metal and glass. Cabin space, always at a premium in the old car, grew appreciably as the project developed. Front seat occupants gained in legroom and the deep-formed sculptured door panels increased elbow room. Headroom grew by 10mm in the front and by no less than 18mm in the rear despite the car actually being reduced in height! This came about by the clever redesign of the floorpan and seating. The proportions of the car changed through the interrelated influence of several factors; aerodynamics, luggage capacity and passive safety requirements. The rear of the car was raised to aid aerodynamics and that in itself increased the boot capacity. The need for increased luggage space suggested an increase in boot length of 95mm which also helped aerodynamics. Capacity went up by 21.8%. The longer rear overhang was visually counterbalanced by the extended front end which in turn helped both aerodynamics and passive safety by adding to the crush zone at the front of the car. All these factors went towards the drag coefficient of 0.38, a vast improvement from the original Scirocco's

0.42. The rear spoiler over the glass hatch not only contributed to this improved drag factor but also helped to cut rear-axle lift by as much as 60%. This was important for high-speed stability as, although the car was well balanced for a front engined/driven car, it only achieved an optimum 50/50 weight distribution when fully laden!

Volkswagen were one of the first European manufacturers to bring a full-size wind tunnel into operation, so they could not make concessions in aerodynamics for the sake of styling. Some of the features that found their way into the final production vehicles certainly were quite innovative. Dispensing with conventional rain gutters was a bold move and the rear window glass running below the spoiler was an interesting design solution that worked very well. In practice, the Scirocco would keep its rear window clear of rain so long as the car kept moving thanks to the airflow management of the car's shape. Aerodynamic reasons also led to the retention of the single wiper-arm introduced with the evolution Scirocco Mk1; it performed better at high speeds in extended tests.

Like the old car, the new Scirocco was introduced with two trim options for its modern, sculptured interior, L/GL and GT. This time though, to broaden the appeal of the car, there were four engines to choose from – 1.3-litre 60bhp, 1.5-litre 70bhp, 1.6-litre 85bhp and 1.6-litre with fuel injection and 110bhp. On the Continent, L, LS, GL and GLS versions were sold with the three carburettor engine options; the GT came with either the 70bhp or 85bhp unit, and the fuel-injected cars were designed GLI and GTI. In the UK, the smallest engine was not offered and the 1.5-litre car, known as the CL, was soon dropped from the line-up as it was very basic, rather underpowered and never sold well. The 1.6 carburettor car was the GLS and, as per the old-shape Scirocco, the fuel-injected car picked up the GTI designation and trim.

The trim levels were instantly recognizable from the front by the large rectangular headlamps on the cheaper cars, with blanking plates on the radiator grille. The GL/GLS/GLI cars had these lights supplemented by smaller, main-beam inner lights and the GT series cars had four smaller but equal-sized rectangular lights. GL-series cars could also be recognized by the bright inserts in their bumpers and roof gutter trim. GT models had the 'Scirocco' name stencilled in the rear glass below the spoiler by way of a white decal. Inside, the GT-trimmed cars had sports seats

The 112bhp 1.8-litre fuel-injected power unit sits well back in the engine bay of the Scirocco Mk2.

There was a successful repeat performance of the Scirocco Storm with the Mk2 car in 1984-5. Exterior colour was either metallic brown or blue.

with special fabric covering and the GTI/GLI cars had a temperature gauge in the centre console. The rear parcel shelf was a one-piece carpet-covered unit in all models except the GTs, where a two-piece vinyl-covered design was used. The extending strings on these did not hold up too well in service and after the 1983 model year, GTI cars adopted the one-piece design from the cheaper versions.

Inside, the new Scirocco was something of a tour de force in its class making the ergonomically good but rather conventional BMW 3-Series

53

Interior of the second-generation Storm was even more lavish than the Mk1 version had been, in an attempt perhaps to steal customers from BMW.

interior look very bland and old-fashioned. Many detail touches were pioneered in the new Scirocco's interior that subsequently became VW styling motifs, appearing in the new Polo and Golf Mk2. The sloping dashboard with its raised instrument binnacle and the prominent centre console bore a passing resemblance to the Porsche 928's interior. It was also one of the first serious attempts in a mass-production car to achieve a style in which the dashboard and door panels looked like an integrated design rather than being on unrelated planes.

Like its predecessor and the Golf Cabriolet, the Scirocco Mk2 was built by Karmann at Osnabruck. In terms of metal thickness, solidity of construction and soundproofing, the new car was streets ahead of both its progenitor and the Golf. Scirocco Mk2 was a beautifully made car that exuded quality and solidity and was a worthy rival to the small BMW in most respects, though it was still a 2+2 rather than a real four-seater.

At the time the Scirocco Mk2 was launched, rival manufacturers like Ford and Vauxhall were upping the ante with their XR3i and Kadett/Astra GTE cars. VW had their 1.8-litre engine in the

pipeline, but as development and testing to make sure everything is totally trouble-free takes time, the new Scirocco GTI had meanwhile to carry nearly 200lb extra weight around with the same 110bhp. Its drag coefficient gave it the edge in top speed and cruising fuel consumption, but acceleration naturally suffered. VW had been experimenting with turbocharging but while performance of the 1.7-litre 178bhp prototype was very impressive, fuel consumption was not and these were still early days in the field of production turbos for passenger cars. Electronic engine management controls were in their youth and something like a Bosch Motronic system was still a year away, quite apart from being too expensive and complex for a car that would have to be affordable to run and share its engine with the cheaper Golf versions. Thus, the 1982 model year was something of a limbo year for VW's new Scirocco in Europe.

In the United States, as before, the Scirocco was only offered with one engine, because of the stringent emission regulations, but in two trim versions. With the extra weight involved, it would have been impossible to use the emasculated 1.6-

litre engine again, especially with even tighter emission laws to be met. Engine capacity was thus increased to 1,715cc by stroking the engine to 86.4mm. On an 8.2:1 compression ratio, the US-spec engine made 74bhp at 5,000rpm and 89.6lb/ft of torque at 3,000rpm. The less stringent Canadian regulations gave the car 2bhp more with 91.3lb/ft of torque. US cars had a 4+E gearbox. Visually, US versions were a mix and match of different European Sciroccos. They had the extended 5mph bumpers but, like the European GL cars, these had bright inserts, which were also seen on the door handles and the rain gutters. Wheels were from the Euro GTI cars and were the nine-spoke pattern introduced on the Golf GTI in 1982 and on the new Scirocco from the beginning. All the US Sciroccos also had the waistline rubber protection strip that was not seen in Europe until the Scirocco GTX and Storm were introduced in 1984/5. At that time, halogen headlamps were still illegal in the US and the cars came with the small rectangular GT-style lights, but to sealed-beam tungsten specification.

In a very sophisticated market where compact cars were dominated by the Japanese, VW offered a very high standard specification. Electric windows, electrically controlled and heated exterior mirrors, power aerial and a stereo radio/cassette were standard equipment on the US-spec Scirocco GL. Options were heavy-duty dampers, air conditioning, de luxe sound system, rear wash/wipe, steel tilt/slide sunroof and heated seats. Interior trim was different from the contemporary European cars and was a subtle check pattern used in the 1983 model year in Europe for the early 1.8-litre GTI cars with the 112bhp engine. The last distinguishing features were the Scirocco decal on the rear window and the lack of any GT or GL flash at the base of the B-pillar. Two years down the line, Wolfsburg special editions and then the 1,781cc versions would wear a Karmann badge there.

For the 1983 model year and coinciding with the introduction of the uprated Golf GTI, the Scirocco at last gained an engine powerful enough to do the rest of the new car justice. With a bore and stroke of 81.0mm x 86.4mm, the 1.8-litre engine was similar to the 1.6-litre in many ways

The Karmann factory in Osnabruck celebrated the production of 600,000 Sciroccos of all types with this 1983½ model-year Limited Edition car.

but was actually a new block and head. The combustion spaces were no longer in the tops of the pistons totally but shared between very slight piston bowls and chambers in the head. Compression ratio went up from 9.5:1 to 10.0:1 and maximum power from 110bhp at 6,100rpm to 112bhp at 5,800rpm. But more significant was the increase in torque from 101lb/ft at 5,000rpm to 109lb/ft at 3,500rpm. The greater torque at lower rpm and the lowering of the maximum engine speed reflected a trend towards greater drivability rather than all-out performance that was gathering momentum and yet, with this new-found power, the Scirocco 1.8-litre was faster in top speed (118mph vs 115mph), faster in acceleration (0-60mph in 8.3sec instead of 9.5sec) and had a significantly better fuel consumption than its smaller brother, reflecting how a bigger engine can often produce better fuel economy figures in a fairly light car as it does not have to be worked so hard. The uprated cars also gained the MFA computer operated by a button on the end of the wiper stalk, and a proper plastic stoneguard instead of a stick-on one for the rear wheelarch. In the 1984 model year, the single wiper arm gave way to a pair, the rear parcel shelf was switched for the GLS style one-piece unit and the cylinder head gained air-shrouded injectors which helped to improve idle and fuel-air mixture preparation. This in turn helped fuel economy.

While the standard 1.8 GTI continued in the UK with just those changes, the Continental European markets were demanding more variations on the basic theme. The body styling kit craze had taken off in a big way and while it was the aftermarket dealers in Britain who were making the money here, Volkswagen itself decided to do a run of special LHD cars with body kits fitted at the factory. Thus, early 1984-spec cars at the end of 1983 included a Scirocco with the Kamei X1 kit fitted and colour-coded to the body colour. Wheels were the 6J x 14in black and silver seven-spoke alloys that appeared a year later on British GTXs which used a different body kit. Concurrent with the Euro-GTX was the GTS version which was a basic GT-spec car with trim like the early Golf GTI 1.8 cars plus large GTS side flashes and body stripes. Wheels were 5½J x 13in steel with 175/70HR13 tyres. Another special available on the Continent in early 1983 was the Scirocco GTS Sprint which had the BBS body kit and 6J x 14in BBS alloys with 185/60HR14 tyres. The GTS and GTS Sprint were offered with the 1.6-litre 85bhp carburetter

engine or the 112bhp injected engine while the GTX was the 1984 model year generation that saw the introduction of the carburettor version of the 1,781cc engine with 90bhp, replacing the smaller unit. This ran alongside the injected engine as an option on the GTX. The GTX used a taller Zender rear spoiler.

Early 1984 was an exciting time for British Scirocco enthusiasts. VAG (UK) Ltd commissioned a successor to the much loved Scirocco Storm Mk1 and imported 700 Mk2 Storms which were available in Cosmos Blue Metallic with blue leather and Havanna Brown Metallic with beige leather. These cars had a full body kit made for VW by Zender Industrieprodukte which was not available in the aftermarket. A new larger tail spoiler which started at the top of the rear hatch on each side of the window helped to balance the effect. 6J x 14in alloys to a new pattern by VW Design were used. These were the wheels later fitted to the Golf GTI 16V and the Scirocco 16V. Inside the Storm, a full leather interior surrounded the occupants in luxury and small touches like wall-to-wall high quality carpeting, leather-trimmed steering wheel and gear knob and a leather gaiter for the gearlever left one in no doubt that this was a compact luxury coupe. How many sales these cars stole from the opposition is unknown but the 700 cars were rapidly sold and a further run was commissioned by customer demand. The Storm was the first Scirocco in any European market to use the black side protection mouldings that the US-spec cars had had since the introduction of the Mk2 car to that market. It was also the first European Scirocco to display Karmann badges on its B-pillars, which were coloured black. GTX cars, incidentally, carried no badges at all on their B-pillars.

1984 was also the model year which saw the introduction of the Golf Mk2. The GTI version followed a few months behind, and in the meantime it was announced that there would be no change to the Scirocco or Golf Cabriolet, and that these Mk1-floorpan-based cars would continue alongside the new car indefinitely.

In the USA, model variations in this period took many cues from Europe. In 1983 VW were beginning to realize that making the Golf in the United States as the Rabbit with a high American content of both ideas and parts was a mistake. Buyers bought VWs because they wanted a German car not an American car. The Cabriolet and Scirocco were imported cars, as was the Jetta, and they had much better street credibility. To boost their flagging image and tempt buyers into the showrooms, VW of America offered special versions of all their cars loaded with goodies and called Wolfsburg Limited-Editions. The 1983 Wolfsburg Limited-Edition Scirocco was the first US-spec car to wear the Karmann badge. In the US, model year change takes place in July and the 1983½ Limited-Edition car had the same Kamei X1 body kit and VW alloy wheels as the German-spec GTX of the 1984 model year. Coincidentally, the 600,000th Scirocco to roll off Karmann's production line, in mid-1983, was one of these cars destined for America.

The Karmann badge stayed on all Sciroccos after that, and with technology catching up with emission laws, the 1983 cars found themselves with the larger European 1,781cc engine, which in US-spec catalytic form produced 90bhp. The 1984½ VW Wolfsburg Limited-Edition Scirocco was an attractive car. A contemporary of the UK market Storm, it had the same blacked-out B-pillars and large rear spoiler but used the multi-finned Passat-style wheels. It also had body colour-coded bumpers and door mirrors, and discreet round badges with the Wolfsburg crest placed just aft of the front wheelarches. This emblem was to characterize all Wolfsburg Specials, and these cars also had the black GT-style VW grille emblem rather than the bright ones used on other US Sciroccos.

The 1985 model year in the UK saw the adoption of the body kit first seen on the Storm for a model that replaced the GTI. Known as the GTX, it was mechanically identical to the GTI and the body kit was left in its semi-matt black plastic finish, and used with a Zender rear spoiler. Fuel tank capacity was now 12 gallons. The cheaper model was now the 1.8-litre 90bhp GTL and the entry level Scirocco was the 75bhp 1.6

GT. In the US market, the car continued without a body kit but the large Storm type rear spoiler was adopted across the range.

June 1985 was the most exciting time for Scirocco enthusiasts since the launch of the new-shape car. After much speculation in the media, the factory 16-valve engine was finally released, and the Golf GTI 16V was accompanied by the Scirocco 16V available in plain or GTX trim. As we have seen, the new engine shared the internal dimensions and block of the eight-valve unit but used a twin-camshaft cylinder head and Bosch KE-Jetronic injection to extract 139bhp at 6,100rpm and 124lb/ft at 4,600rpm. A catalytic convertor-equipped version for countries like Switzerland, and indeed Germany itself, produced the same torque 350rpm lower down the scale and 129bhp at 6,000rpm. The suspension was up-graded with a lower strut brace tying the front wishbones, as well as uprated springs, dampers and anti-roll bars. Larger, ventilated disc brakes were used at the front with solid discs at the back. The alloy wheels on both 16V Golfs and Sciroccos were the VW Design style first seen on the UK-only Scirocco Storm and were of 6J x 14in dimensions with 185/60VR14 tyres. The black body kit was identical to the GTX cars but with the Storm/USA-style rear spoiler. All 16V cars had a radio aerial mounted at the rear of the roof, a position chosen to provide better screening from the high-output electronic ignition system.

The 16V engine brought a new level of performance to the Scirocco. The top speed was 129mph (which this writer was able to verify during the press launch by running to the red line on the rev counter on a flat stretch of autobahn) and the 0-60mph time was 7.6 seconds. High-speed stability was excellent, the larger spoilers offering extra downforce without affecting the

For European markets, a Kamei body kit – front and rear aprons and sill extensions – was fitted to produce the Scirocco GTX.

Close-up of the rear end of the Kamei-equipped Scirocco GTX.

For 1984 onwards, a body kit made by Zender exclusively for VW was used on the GTX. Colour-coded, this kit was also used on the Storm and Scala limited-run versions.

Every year, VW of America commission specially equipped versions of VW models in limited quanties. This is a 1984½ Wolfsburg Limited Edition Scirocco.

Rear end of the Scirocco 16V showing the distinctive twin exhausts which went with the multi-valve power unit.

State of the art: the 1987 Scirocco GT. Current policy is that the Scirocco will continue to occupy its market niche and not be replaced by the Corrado.

drag coefficient which remained at 0.38. Although the Golf Mk2 had a 0.34Cd, its frontal area was larger, accounting for the fact that both cars had a CdA of 0.68m^2. The 16V was also the first Scirocco to offer power-assisted steering as an option.

The US version of the 16V arrived nearly a year later as a 1986½ model. In this specification, the car had 123bhp at 5,800rpm and 120lb/ft at 4,250rpm. Top speed was 122mph but the car would still turn an 8.1sec 0-60mph time. These cars made up one third of the 1986 US-market Scirocco production and were offered in Flash Silver, Tornado Red or black. The body kit was colour-coded and standard equipment included a stainless steel exhaust, alloy wheels of a flat teardrop design, and electric mirrors.

In the UK, the Scirocco 16V was only offered to special order, in left-hand-drive form, and consequent low sales numbers make this ultimate Scirocco a relative rarity. For the 1986 model year, British-market Scirocco GTX cars inherited the centre console-mounted voltmeter from the 16V in place of the oil temperature gauge, gained a split folding rear seat, Pirelli-designed alloy wheels as per the Campaign Golf GTI Mk1s, and green tinted, heat-insulating glass. The large 16V-style rear spoiler became standard and the model range was rationalized to the 75bhp 1.6-litre GT, the 112bhp GTX and the special order 16V. The GT version shared the same body addenda but ran on steel wheels. A limited-edition 90bhp GTS Scirocco was produced that year and had a colour-coded body kit and Pirelli alloy wheels.

The colour-coded body kit became the norm in 1987 with just the GT versions of all engine types in Europe wearing the kit in black. The GTX cars with 90bhp and 112bhp used the black and silver seven-spoke wheels, the GTX 16V cars used the Scirocco Storm/16V alloys and a new fabric trim was introduced with leather still an option. The Scirocco Scala made its debut in 1988 and this was offered across Europe, including the UK. These cars were very much like the previous year's GTX models but had colour-coded interior trim, and the non-polished parts of the seven spoke wheels were colour-coded to the body. A new colour range was introduced for 1989 along with a model known as the Scirocco GT II. This used the 6J x 14in steel wheels and trims from the Golf Driver, chequered fabric trim, and shared the new range of emission-controlled engines produced to meet the latest EC 15.05 regulations. Thus the 1.6-litre car now had 72bhp and the fuel-injected engine dropped its power to practically US-spec with just 95bhp using a three-way catalytic convertor and Lambda sensor. The Scala versions shared these power units, although Britain and Italy, still tied to EC 15.04, continued to use the 'dirty' 112bhp engine. The 16V engine disappeared from the 1989 model-year line-up upon introduction of the Corrado, VW's new coupe flagship. The Scirocco GT II and Scala remain in production as VW's entry level coupe through the 1990 model year, and the deleted 16V has become a very sought-after used car.

In the USA, the Scirocco was absent from the 1989 model year line-up in all its forms. VW did not introduce the Corrado into this market until October 1989 for the 1990 model year and then only in G60 form.

3

Born to run: Corrado

Volkswagen has always wanted to build a sports car. Porsche has used VW components in some of its cars for a long time but VW has wanted its own sports car for over two decades now. In the late 1960s, the two companies joined forces and the unlovely Porsche 914 was the result. Another co-operative venture in the mid-1970s spawned the 924, launched in November 1975, the same year as the Golf. This car was originally a VW project but after the Board killed it in the wake of the oil crisis in 1973, it was handed over to Porsche to be completed. This explains why the Porsche 924 was produced at the Audi-NSU plant at Neckarsulm where 944s too were made until recently. VW goes to great pains to call the Corrado a sports car rather than a coupe, but in truth, this sleek three-door car based on the Golf Mk2 floorpan fits the definition of a coupe more closely. Sports cars after all do not carry four adults in comfort and all their luggage.

Journalists who caught a glimpse of Corrado (Spanish for 'Sprinter') prototypes mistakenly called it 'Taifun'. The Taifun programme was in fact run until 1983 and was a design study for a similar-sized car but with a square back like the Lancia HPE or Honda Aerodeck. The Corrado was the work of VW Design under Herbert Schafer, and some sources have hinted that the car costs more than was originally intended because quality and performance were judged more important than cost monitoring. In the event, the notion that the Corrado would supplant the Scirocco as VW's Golf-based sporty coupe was thus altered and the Scirocco will continue in production for as long as there is a healthy demand for this value-for-money coupe. With

history thus irrevocably changed, the fastest and most expensive VW ever made entered the marketplace almost midway between the Golf GTI 16V and what was then the entry-level Porsche 944 2.5-litre, both in price and perceived status. Introduced just after the demise of the Porsche 924S, the Corrado was seen as a worthy car to fill that vacant slot, perhaps ironically fulfilling VWs age-old wish to put a sporting car into that area of the market.

To an onlooker, the Corrado bears many similarities in its bodyshell architecture to the original Scirocco as penned by Giugiaro. There would be nothing unusual about this if the Corrado were in fact a Scirocco replacement, as many VW enthusiasts prefer the sharper looks of the Mk1 to the more rounded VW-designed successor. Schafer denies such visual references though and considers the long nose, wide C-pillars and lipped wheelarches as being traditional VW styling elements. Dissect the styling of the Corrado, and you will indeed find this to be true, but the real angel in the architecture is an element that has never before manifested itself in a VW design. Most classic car designs, especially those from Italy, tend to hinge around one base line from which the rest of the car emanates. Look at a Ferrari 246GT or a 308/328 GTB and you will see what I mean: the sweeping line that arcs its way from the front bumper to the top of the Kamm tail is its backbone. Look at the Corrado and you will see the same kind of wave form in action. It gives a car a dynamism, a life of its own even when it is standing still, that is missing from one with just straight or flaccid rounded lines.

The question has also been asked why the

Dynamic form: Volkswagen's body design for the Corrado was a very accomplished piece of styling, combining sweeping lines with a taut, compact shape. An absence of non-functional frills and a sturdy, crouching stance make the car look powerful even at rest. No mere cosmetic coupe, the Corrado is a grand tourer in its own right.

Corrado engine compart-
ments, in normally-aspirated
16-valve form, above, and
the G60 version with supercharger, right. The 136bhp
16-valve engine is only
offered in the UK and Italy
where emission laws are less
strict. Other European
countries get the 160bhp G60
version and the US cars have
158bhp.

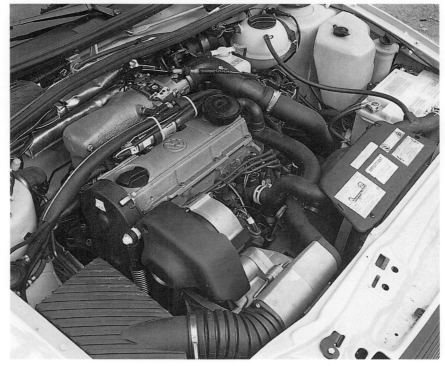

The dashboard of the Corrado shares many elements with the third-generation Passat, but its wraparound design is highly suitable for a sporty coupe.

Corrado has such a conventional front grille when the latest Passat saloon, which shares the rear axle and dashboard with it, has a very aerodynamic nose cone. The answer is that sports car buyers tend to prefer classical shapes and the intention with the Passat was to take a bold step away from competitors in the mid-sized saloon market. Schafer explained that the front of the car, and the headlamp treatment in particular, caused a lively debate amongst the design team. Pop-up head-lamps were rejected on grounds of performance and because it was felt they did not match the car's purpose. The final design suits the car but has not done the drag coefficient any favours. 0.32 is good, but not spectacularly so, when you consider the 0.29 achieved by the Passat saloon. CdA is a respectable $0.58m^2$

The high sweeping tail of the car looks good and benefits both aerodynamics and luggage capacity, but it is detrimental to rearward vision. It would be even worse if the rear aerofoil were a permanent fixture, but this device, which cuts rear wheel lift at speed by 64%, is only extended to its

50mm additional height when the car reaches 75mph. This has been reduced to 45mph for the UK market and there is a manual over-ride button. The Corrado is the first production VW to get fully integrated colour-coded bumpers from the word go. If your rear passengers are sma adults then the car is a true four-seater. Peop over average height reduce it to a generous 2+2 rear headroom is lacking. Having said that, it is a vast improvement on the Scirocco and is capable of doubling as a long-distance touring car for a small family. When all is said and done, then, Corrado works out as a worthy Grand Touring car. Forget the arguments about sports car or coupe; it is a GT car in the best Italian tradition.

The comfortable interior of the car reflects this too. The sports seats with their figure-hugging raised sides are finished in high-quality, subtly patterned cloth or leather and hold you well in hard cornering. A fixed central armrest divides the two back seats, making the car a four seater. The squabs are raked to make full use of available leg and headroom and the seat back is a split

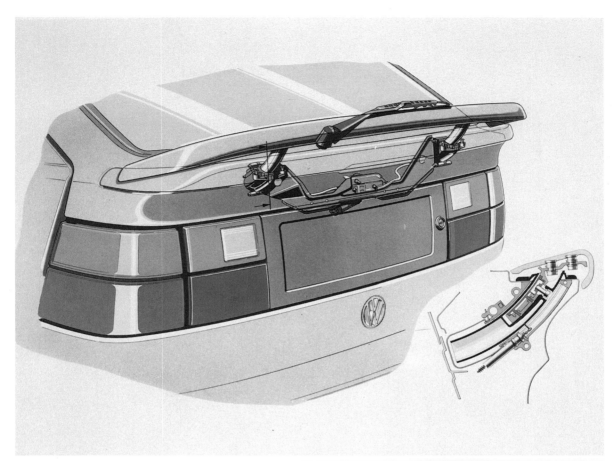

Operating mechanism for the retractable rear spoiler, above. Time-lapse photograph, right, illustrates its action from rest to fully extended at speed.

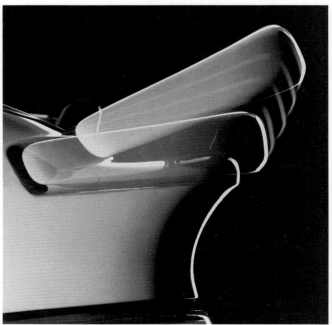

Rear axle of the Corrado, also used for the Passat, showing the special trailing-arm bushes which provide passive rear-wheel steering.

folding design that turns the car into a generous load carrier and it can carry long loads selectively with its 60/40 folding capability. Passat owners will recognize the dashboard and instrument panel. Perhaps VW could have been more imaginative here, but the design works well from an ergonomic point of view and the wraparound look suits the sporting bias of the car. Pre-production cars had a voltmeter and temperature gauge in the lowest quadrant of the centre console, but this was not carried through to the production cars and the space behind it is just an extra cubbyhole that could be filled with a Fischer C-Box cassette holder, or indeed extra instruments. At last, a Karmann badge appears on the inside of a production VW. After years of making Golf Cabriolets and Sciroccos for VW, Karmann has been given the green light to put a badge on the rear of the centre console between the gearlever and handbrake. A small point, but one that

reinforces the Corrado's status as a coachbuilt GT car, albeit a mass-produced one.

After the pretty dismal provision for good quality audio speakers in previous VWs, the Corrado's interior does give music buffs the possibility of fitting fairly decent equipment. The door speaker pods are built into the door pockets, but will take 5½in speakers, and there is provision for tweeters on top of the dashboard if you are so inclined. The rear parcel shelf supports contain small speakers and you would have to reinforce the shelf itself to fit sub-woofers.

While the floorpan of the Corrado is derived from the Golf Mk2, the suspension detail changes which incorporate ideas and experience from the new Passat have taken it into a different league in terms of handling and poise. The MacPherson strut and coil spring front suspension of the Golf GTI 16V is carried over unchanged apart from basic spring and damper rate alterations to cope

Corrado 16V at speed. Handling and performance of the car are impressive and totally in tune with its looks.

with a car that is nearly 400lb heavier dry. It is the rear end, however, which has benefited from the Passat's updated rear-axle configuration. Still a torsion-beam design as used by VW since the first Golf, this new rear axle incorporates passive rear-wheel steer through the use of track-correcting bearings that react to cornering forces. VW investigated active 4WS of the kind that the Japanese have productionized and concluded that the passive system was much less complex and therefore more reliable in the long term as well as costing less to produce. A passive system may not have the advantages of easier manoeuvring in parking situations but VW felt quite correctly that 4WS in any form should primarily be there to promote active safety by making a car more stable in cornering.

Power-assisted rack-and-pinion steering is fitted to all Corrados but the braking arrangements differ. The 1.8-litre 16-valve cars use 256mm front discs, while the more powerful G60 cars, which have Bosch ABS anti-lock brakes as standard, have larger, 280mm diameter brakes. Both models use 15in diameter alloy wheels, but there is a choice of ordering 195/50VR15 tyres on $6^{1}/_{2}$J x 15in BBS three-piece spoked wheels if you feel the 185/55VR15 rubber on the standard 6J x 15in VW alloys is not adequate.

There are two engines available in the Corrado, the 1.8-litre 16-valve or the G60 supercharged eight-valve unit, but the former is only made for the British and Italian markets as it is a 'dirty' engine that complies to the ECE 15.04 emission regulations but not the forthcoming tighter rules that require catalytic convertors. Catalyst-equipped 16-valve engines have 129bhp rather than 139bhp in the Golf GTI 16V, and in the Corrado the different installation and exhaust causes a loss of 3bhp and 5lb/ft of torque. That means the Corrado 16V has 136bhp at 6,300rpm

Sprinter on the beach: Corrado 16V at rest on Pendine Sands.

and 119lb/ft at 4,800rpm compared to 139bhp at 6,100rpm and 124lb/ft at 4,600rpm. In catalyst form, the cumulative power loss would be such that, coupled with the fact that the Corrado is nearly 400lb heavier than the Golf, the car would be badly underpowered.

Thus, in all other markets, only the super-charged car is sold. With the G-charger and an 8.0:1 compression ratio, the eight-valve engine makes 160bhp at 5,600rpm and 165lb/ft of torque at 4,000rpm. In USA spec with three-way catalytic convertor, the peak power drops 2bhp. Given the power losses and extra weight, the Corrado 16V does not do badly in the performance stakes. The final drive is the same as the Golf GTI 16V's at 3.67:1 and indeed all gear ratios save for first are the same. The Golf 16V/Scirocco 16V's first gear is 3.45:1 and the Corrado's is 3.40:1, a minimal difference to help the car off the line. With two on board, the Corrado will still reach 60mph from rest in 8.53sec and pass 100mph in 23.5sec. That

is 0.6sec and 1.5sec behind the figures I obtained for a 16V Golf. Aerodynamics see to it that top speed is higher, though, and a best one-way maximum of 132mph was seen compared to 129mph for the GTI.

With a lot more power and torque on tap, the G60 Corrado is quicker than the 16-valve car, but not dramatically so. For those who think 160bhp is a lot, a 0-60mph times of 8.0sec sounds dis-appointing. But the true worth of the super-charger is in providing torque and flexibility, as the 40-100mph times in fourth and fifth gears prove. In fourth, the 16V takes 32sec to bridge this speed range which is covered in just 23.6sec by the G60. In fifth, the same speeds are covered in 42.9sec and 32.7sec respectively by the two cars, showing how much more flexible the G60 engine is. The top speed of the G60 Corrado is an impressive 138.7mph, which makes the car as fast as a 1987 Porsche 944 or an Audi quattro.

4

GTI in South Africa

South Africa is a performance-car enthusiasts' paradise. The local representatives of manufacturers like BMW and Ford have, over the years, come up with their own home-grown derivatives of European models that would leave enthusiasts in Europe green with envy. Back in the mid-1980s when the fastest BMWs in Europe in their respective ranges were the 323i and 745i, the former of 150bhp and the latter a turbocharged 3.2-litre 252bhp autobahn stormer, BMW of South Africa were somewhat more adventurous and installed the 3.2-litre straight-six in the 3-Series body to produce the 197bhp 333i. While BMW AG had yet to spawn the 24-valve 286bhp M5, BMW SA took this M1-derived power unit for their version of the 745i flagship.

Down the road at Ford, V6 Essex-engined Cortinas and Granadas were being supplemented by locally developed V8-powered versions of these cars, and the ultimate fast Ford was made in 1985/6 – the Sierra XR8 homologation special. This five-door Sierra with its RS alloys and XR4i tailgate biplane spoiler packed a 5.0-litre SVO V8 engine of 206bhp under its rep's car bonnet. It also had seriously uprated suspension and huge ventilated racing discs with four-pot calipers all round.

If this is what other manufacturers were doing at the time, Volkswagen of South Africa was just pulling itself out of the doldrums. A wholly owned subsidiary of VW AG, VWSA was the market leader in 1979/80 following the local launch of the Golf the year before. The company's market share was around 20%. Unfortunately, quality control problems in the local factory saw this share evaporate by half in the ensuing four years. In the

face of a declining car market in the country as a whole, VWSA set about rebuilding its image, and from 1985 onwards it has been the only local car manufacturer to increase market share every year.

When the first Golfs rolled off the production lines in 1978, knowledge of the GTI version in Europe prompted development of a local performance derivative. This turned out to be a five-door car with similar trim and instrumentation to the GTI but powered by an 86bhp carburettor version of the 1.6-litre engine. It was dubbed the Golf GTS. The Golf GTS was a resounding success and this prompted VWSA to introduce their GTi in 1983. As this coincided with the 1983 model year in Europe, which introduced the 1,800cc engine, the original GTI 1.6-litre was never sold in South Africa. Having said that, two years previously, the company imported 100 each of the Golf GLi Cabriolet and Scirocco GLi, and these cars are very sought after on the used car market today. The VWSA GTi Mk1's suspension was adapted for local conditions which vary from good quality tarmac to dirt roads. The cars ended up with firmer suspension and more ground clearance to cope. The shock absorbers were locally sourced, as the German ones were felt to be too firm for local conditions. Standard footwear was 175/70HR13 steel-belted radials on locally made alloy wheels.

The South African GTI was and still is badged 'GTi'. From the word go, the cars have had a higher specification than their European counterparts, with a four-headlamp grille and alloy wheels appearing on all versions including the early GTS cars. All have also been with five-door bodyshells. The latest Mk2 cars have still not

South African GTi has the lower case 'i' but is a real GTI in every other way, with four-headlamp grille, alloy wheels and colour-coded bumpers and wheelarch spats.

adopted the centrally positioned rear VW logo on either Golf or Jetta. As in Europe, a leather trim option is available but this is full-leather rather than just the seats, and is standard on the top-of-the-range GTi 16V Executive, along with power steering, air conditioning, central locking, Pioneer stereo, electric windows and mirrors, alloy wheels and a four-spoke leather-bound Italvolanti sports steering wheel. In 1984, the Jetta GLi was introduced to the market and, as in Europe, this model shared the GTi's mechanical specification. It differed from European GLi models in having exactly the same interior trim as the GTi.

With motorsport being very popular in South Africa, the GTi was soon well established in the

Golf GTi Mk2 in action, showing the colour-coded bumpers, small reflectors under the indicator lights and the multi-spoke alloy wheels used in the South African market.

Interior of the GTi has locally made Recaro-style seats in half-leather and a four-spoke Italvolanti steering wheel.

production saloon racing and rallying series, winning a number of championships. By now VWSA was catching up fast with new European models, and, bolstered by sales successes, it introduced the Golf Mk2 at the end of 1984, soon after the car's European debut. The GTi version followed in early 1985 and this came with 6J x 14in locally made alloy wheels and 185/60HR14 tyres. The Golf GTS was reincarnated in Mk2 form, again using a carburettor version of the GTi motor. This gave 85bhp instead of the 112bhp produced by the fuel-injected version, and the interior trim of the GTS was identical to the GTi's apart from deletion of the MFA computer. Externally, though, you could tell the GTS at a glance as it had 13in diameter steel wheels.

Suspension of the VWSA Mk2 car once again used locally made springs and dampers. When the 16-valve version was introduced in August 1986, the German suspension settings and ground clearance were judged too harsh and low for local conditions, so the same suspension as the eight-valve cars was used. The exhaust system on VWSA Mk1 cars is the same as the Wolfsburg-built cars, but the Mk2s use a reverse-flow stainless-steel muffler design which gives a slightly higher back pressure. Despite this, power outputs are unchanged. The exhaust pipes are also made of stainless steel as the German ones corrode through in about 18 months in South African conditions. The tailpipes of this stainless-steel system are larger, but exhaust manifolds are the same as the German ones. There is as yet no requirement for catalytic convertors in South Africa.

Other local modifications include a dust sealing package, right-hand-drive wiper pattern locally tooled since 1978, and, from 1988, all Golf 2s have come with a factory-fitted security alarm with an auto-arming immobilizer. This is activated by a coded transmission from a key-ring transmitter which is tied into the central locking,

One of the prominent VW tuners is Steve's Auto Clinic who modified this Jetta CLi 16V. The body kit is by Zender and the 7J x 15in wheels are from MIM in Italy.

standard on all GTi versions. Cost reasons prohibit the use of the Recaro seats that are an option in Europe, and the sports seats found in VWSA cars are not the same as the German ones even though they appear outwardly similar. All GTi cars also have leather gearshift gaiters.

The Jetta equivalents are badged as 'CLi'. There are three models – the CLi, CLi Executive and CLi 16V Executive. The CLi has the eight-valve 112bhp engine and comes with central locking, leather steering wheel, sports seats, electric mirrors, alloy wheels and Pioneer stereo standard; the CLi Executive specification adds power steering, electric windows and air conditioning to that, and the 16V has all of these additions plus the trim from the Golf GTi. All the South African cars used the Scirocco Mk1 (1978-81) three-spoke type steering wheel up till 1986 when the Golf GTi adopted the European Polo Coupe GT wheel and the Jettas used a leather-bound version of the European GTi four-spoke factory wheel. 16V cars use the Italvolanti leather sports wheel. Digifant electronic injection does not feature on VWSA's cars at all. Current eight-valve cars still use the Bosch K-Jetronic system and of course the 16Vs have the KE-Jetronic.

Neither the Scirocco nor the Corrado has been

or will be available in South Africa. The local content regulations are very stringent and, as production numbers are fairly small, it is not economically viable to undertake local manufacture of these cars, while the very high import duties would make the cost of importation prohibitive.

An interesting hybrid car still in production is the Citi Golf Sport. This popular, entry level Golf is the spiritual successor to the original Mk1 GTi and has a 1,781cc carburettor-fed engine with 95bhp. Built in five-door form with locally re-engineered bumpers and grille, it is a hot seller to enthusiasts who cannot quite afford a GTi, and is really a car somewhere between the European Golf Driver and the GTi.

Late in 1990, VWSA will relaunch the GTi Mk1 as a properly sorted car with all the original weak points like the poor brakes on RHD cars engineered out. This car will use the 112bhp injected 1,800cc engine and carry the designation 'Citi Golf CTi'. Available in five-door form only, it will have a restyled front and rear and be totally colour-coded apart from the GTi-style black decal around the rear window. Front and rear spoilers will be part of the package along with three extra instruments in the centre console. The proposed alloy wheels are of a similar design to

VW of South Africa are enthusiastic tuners themselves and built this 'Concept' GTi in 1986 with a Hella body kit and BBS wheels.

those on the Audi V8 but of 6J x 14in size with 65-series tyres.

Also on the cards for 1990 is a 2-litre 16-valve engine for the Golf and Jetta, using the new Passat block. While this engine produces just 136bhp in Euro catalytic form, the lack of stringent emission laws in South Africa allows the engineers to tune the unit for power. High up on the reef, all the naturally aspirated engines lose 17 to 20% of their power, so the ability to use the bigger engine is most welcome. Also, the 2-litre 16-valve Opel Kadetts have been having it their own way in Group N racing in recent months, so VWSA

decided to fight back. The first 2-litre cars will be 16-valve Executive specification Golfs and Jettas with emphasis on luxury rather than speed. High torque is the main consideration, and the engines will be limited to 150bhp. Group N racing is a serious target for the 2-litre model, though, and a limited run of 500 sports models with no air conditioning or power steering will come later, along with 200 stripped for use in the championship. These cars will be tuned for over 170bhp, which should be enough to give the Opels a nasty fright. As we noted in the beginning, South Africa is a performance-car enthusiasts' paradise.

5

Engineers extraordinary

The Development Department at Wolfsburg is a constant hive of activity, designing and building prototypes as part of the continuing process of exploring new concepts and new extensions of established ones. Wolfsburg's projects tend in the main to be engineering led rather than influenced by market demands, whereas many other companies, especially the Japanese, are marketing led. Volkswagen see the danger of creating or responding to fashions that pass quickly, and endeavour instead to base their vehicles on ideas and technology that are both practical and long lasting. A good example is the innovation of four-wheel steering: while the Japanese manufacturers have gone for expensive and complex active systems that may be unpredictable if you overstep the limits of roadholding and could be problematic in the car's later life, VW have opted for a simple but effective passive system for the Passat and Corrado. Much of the Development Department's work, inevitably, remains confidential. But some fascinating vehicles have been revealed, and they illustrate well the combination of bold experimentation and sound practicality which characterizes VW.

Turbo Scirocco
Soon after the launch of the 1.8-litre engine, VW engineers were working on the next round of power increases for the GTI family. One of the possibilities explored was turbocharging. This was an ongoing project, because the 1.6-litre engine had been turbocharged in trials in 1981, before the Scirocco Mk2 was launched. VW knew the car was too heavy for the 1.6-litre engine and were looking for alternatives. In the event, the boosted engine proved to be heavy on fuel and created heat problems that VW found unacceptable for a production car.

The 1983 car was based on the US-spec 1.7-litre engine, had 178bhp and was capable of 138mph. The body styling was a mix of the Kamei side skirts and rear valance as used on the GTX of that model year with the Zender front spoiler that was undergoing trials for the 1984 model-year GTX. This was because the flatter front of the Zender spoiler allowed a cut-out to be made for the intercooler that was placed low down across the front of the car. Concurrently, VW's own 16-valve head was being developed and of course that was the route chosen for the next generation of high-performance engines. But the existence of the turbo car, taken to an advanced state of development, shows that more than one option is thoroughly explored at Wolfsburg before a decision is made.

Twin engines
While the turbo Sciroccos were not too far from the high-street world of production cars, some other radical vehicles were made which pushed back the boundary between reality and fantasy yet continued to use existing technology. The twin-engined cars – there were several versions – are described later when we look at VW Motorsport, for it was that department which instigated the idea and built the Twin-Jet Jetta and the first twin-engined Scirocco. Dr Ulrich Seiffert of the Development Department took the Bimotor Scirocco a stage further, though, using two Oettinger 16-valve engines each rated at 141bhp at 6,100rpm and 124lb/ft of torque at 5,500rpm.

Development cars like this early Scirocco Mk2 often wore special body addenda and wheels. This particular car was turbocharged as part of VW's investigation of that form of tuning, later abandoned in favour of supercharging.

The Bimotor Scirocco was developed from earlier VW Motorsport twin-engined cars and was finished up to production-car standards.

The See-Golf was the most amazing project ever undertaken by the Development Department. It had retractable pontoons for buoyancy and propeller drive powered by a supercharged GTI engine. Maybe there would have been a market for this ultimate leisure vehicle amongst Germany's 700,000 windsurfers!

The weight distribution of the car was almost perfectly 50:50.

See-Golf

The most outrageous vehicle ever to escape from the Development Department was the See-Golf. The brainchild of Professor Ernst Fiala, the See-Golf was intended to increase technical knowledge about the behaviour of a normal road engine when used for propulsion on water where it would run with maximum load and minimum cooling. The engine was supercharged by VW Motorsport to give it between 150bhp and 170bhp, depending on boost pressure, and 137lb/ft of torque at 5,000rpm. The See-Golf had a modified differential with a propshaft take-off that allowed it to drive a four-bladed propeller at the rear. A rudder was added to provide steering in the water. The two huge pontoons that provided flotation were hydraulically raised and lowered. The See-Golf had a top speed of 20 knots in the water and an amphibious range of about 25 miles. It is now in the VW AutoMuseum in Wolfsburg.

IRVW 3

IRVW stands for Integrated Research VW and, unlike many concept cars, this 1985 Jetta-based vehicle was built to show a combination of safety, performance and comfort features that could well appear in family cars in the not too distant future. Five years on, we can see how many of these features have indeed found their way into production VWs: a supercharged 1.8-litre engine; five-speed gearbox that automatically changes up from fourth to fifth for fuel saving; ASR, an anti-slip device to control wheelspin on slippery surfaces; ABS anti-lock braking; air suspension for a better ride and which drops the ride height of the car for high-speed driving; a fully adjustable seat-belt system to cater for all sizes of driver and passenger; and an on-board navigation computer.

The IRVW 3's engine produced 180bhp at 5,500rpm and 175lb/ft at 4,000rpm on 1.7-bar boost. The fuel injection/management was the Digijet system to be seen on production cars from 1988. The car could sprint to 60mph in 7.1 seconds, covered the 50-70mph gap in 7.8 seconds in fourth gear and had a maximum speed of 132.5mph.

IRVW 3 was a very sophisticated mid-size saloon with the ride and performance of a luxury limousine.

VW Motorsport

In 1991, VW Motorsport will celebrate its 25th anniversary; 25 successful years of preparing VW-based vehicles that have competed against and often beaten the best that other manufacturers have fielded in tarmac or loose-surface motorsport. It all started in 1966 with Formula V in Europe, and through 1970 (when Formula Super V made its debut) to 1976 this competition offshoot of normal factory operations was concerned purely with open-wheeled VW-engined racing cars. This changed with the launch of the Golf and Scirocco, and in 1976, the VW Junior Cup came into being, a one-make championship for the newly introduced GTI version of the Scirocco. The aim of the championship was to create publicity for the new car by proving its durability, speed and handling in near-standard form. A year later, the Golf GTI took the Scirocco's place in the Championship and the Golf was further developed for rally duties in Group 1b. By 1980, Golf GTIs were taking part in Group 1 and 2 in various rallies and with the Alfons Stock/Paul Schmuck team at the helm, a Group 2 GTI won the 1981 German Rally Championship.

This year was also significant for two other reasons. Firstly, it witnessed the public debut of a 16-valve GTI in a factory car. This was a Group 4 rally car equipped with the Oettinger 16-valve cylinder head. To qualify for competition, the cylinder head had to be homologated through the certified production of 400 road cars. This was easy enough to do as the French market at that time was taking over 50% of its Golf sales as GTIs and the threat to the GTI 1.6 from other, newer hot hatchbacks meant that the French importer was searching for a more powerful version.

Twin-Jet Jetta

The second surprise to emerge from the VW Motorsport workshops was their answer to the Audi quattro in the form of a twin-engined Jetta. This prototype, affectionately known as the Twin-Jet, was painted banana yellow with a colour-coded grille and had a headlamp set-up similar to the US-market version. A body kit with intergrated front spoiler and over-bumper sections that blended into the extended wheel-arches gave the car a more purposeful look and covered the 205/60VR-13 Pirelli P7R tyres that were supported by 6J x 13in ATS alloy wheels. The Twin-Jet was the brainchild of Klaus-Peter Rosorius, Head of VW Motorsport since 1972,

A line-up of Scirocco Cup racers. The spoilers are from Zender and the wheels by ATS.

The Twin-Jet Jetta was painted a lurid bright yellow and wore a modified BBS body styling kit.

and Kurt Bergmann from Vienna, one-time builder of all-conquering FV cars. The idea was a bit of a wild card in the pack, but Rosorius was determined to pull it off as a good PR exercise even if it did not work as a rally car. Because the Jetta has a transversely mounted engine, it was necessary to have another complete drivetrain package at the rear, whereas had the engine been mounted north-south, a single gearbox could have been used. In the event, the underbonnet structure from a second Jetta was spliced in to a reinforced boot area. This gave the car a rear suspension identical to the front save for the use of Heim-jointed tubular lower arms in place of the front-end's pressed steel arms. A new heavy-duty anti-roll bar was made up for the rear to balance things out, and a pair of front ventilated discs joined the rear axle assembly. As things were arranged, you could choose from front drive, rear drive or four-wheel drive, so a brake proportioning control was mounted on the transmission tunnel. The handbrake had hydraulic actuation.

The two power plants were standard 110bhp 1,588cc GTI units and the Twin-Jet thus had a combined thrust of 220bhp at 6,100rpm and 202lb/ft of torque at 5,000rpm. The ignition and fuel systems ran independently of one another, but a large capacity radiator served both engines and this was supplemented by an additional electric fan at the rear. While the gearboxes were standard Jetta GLI close-ratio five-speeders, the final drive was raised from 3.90:1 to 3.70:1 to make full use of the greater power in top speed terms. A limited-slip differential was incorporated into the rear transaxle. The kerb weight of the car was just 2,310lb compared to the 2,046lb of a normal Jetta GLI. With superb traction in 4WD configuration, this gave the car very impressive performance and, in truth, the car worked out far better than its builders had hoped. In 12,000 development miles, covered in just a few months after it was built in 1981, the Twin-Jet spurred Rosorius into giving the go-ahead for a twin-engined version of the just-launched Scirocco Mk2.

Bimotor Scirocco
With the twin-engined formula working successfully in the Jetta with standard engines, VW Motorsport were confident enough now to shoot for the limits of the drivetrain's capability with the twin-engined Scirocco. The new 1,781cc engine slated for 1983 model-year production was not yet available, so VW Motorsport asked its contract engine builder, Eckhart Berg, to increase the bore and stroke of the existing 1.6-litre engine to

The twin-engined Scirocco in action. It was a fully operational prototype and would have made a fine rally car.

achieve the larger capacity. With a bore and stroke of 81.25mm x 86.4mm, the larger engine worked out at 1,791cc and the twin engines were thus equivalant to a 3.58-litre eight-cylinder unit. Internally, forged pistons and reworked combustion chambers increased the compression ratio to 10.9:1 and, with hotter camshafts, the output of each engine was 180bhp at 7,200rpm with 148lb/ft of torque at 5,800rpm. Helping to achieve this was a Zenith Pierburg racing fuel-injection system with one throttle body per cylinder. These were basically rallycross-spec motors.

Two twin-engined Sciroccos were to be built, one for evaluation and testing and another to do shows and the like. The first car was also built to convince the VW Board of the potential of the car, and it just happened to have 54bhp more than the Audi Sport quattro rally homologation special, which it equalled in acceleration and bettered in top speed, through taller gearing. VW Motorsport and Audi Sport were run as two distinct and separate departments and one detects an element of rivalry between them spurring the VW engineers on, for it was the Audi branch that was getting all the limelight in international rallying at this period.

The power was fed through a pair of single-plate sintered-metal clutches to identical five-speed gearboxes. Each end of the car had a limited-slip differential and, if a high final-drive ratio was opted for, the theoretical top speed was close to 180mph. In the event, the car ran with a short final drive and this gave it blistering acceleration. 0-60mph took a mere 4.5 seconds, enough to embarrass a Porsche 911 Turbo. 100mph followed 7 seconds after that and the quarter-mile trap closed on the car in 13 seconds.

Perhaps the most ingenious feature of the twin-engined Scirocco was the way the engines were synchronised. Given the title 'E-gas', which means electronic hookup, the linking system was deceptively simple. A single throttle cable ran back to the rear engine where a potentiometer measured throttle position and sent a signal forward to operate a valve on the other engine. While the Scirocco retained the ability of the Jetta to run on front, rear or both engines, it had the additional refinement of a slide-operated throttle potentiometer which adjusted front engine power and thus the front-rear power split. The car was hardly nose heavy with a good 52.6/47.4% front/rear weight distribution, but even so it was a great advantage to be able to dial in different handling characteristics at will, especially when it came to countering understeer on loose surfaces. The gearboxes were mechanically linked by rods and cranks, with a small pneumatically operated plunger device connecting each of these assemblies near the gearbox to lock out one or the other shift mechanism in the event of a single engine failure.

The bodyshell modifications were different from those of the twin-motor Jetta. A suitable hole was cut in the shell to accept the rear drivetrain which had to be angled forward from the rear axle line. The other modifications followed the proven formula used on the Twin-Jet however, and Bilstein dampers were used together with adjustable suspension, and 10.5in vented disc brakes all round with four-pot racing calipers. The wheels were 7J x 15in Centra alloys shod with 205/50VR15 Pirelli P7s.

The second Bimotor Scirocco was a rather different animal. The project was now in the hands of Dr Ulrich Seifert at VW's Development Department and this metallic red car was brought to a state of finish where it could have been put into limited production. The car wore a specially moulded body kit which encompassed front and rear bumpers, and quattro-style wheelarch flares with engine intake grilles let into the leading edge of the rear ones. (Wheels were from an early Audi quattro.) The twin exhaust pipes at the rear were neatly centred in semi-circular cutouts rather than simply protruding from the bodywork. Open the rear hatch, and the standard of finish continued to impress. The engine compartment surround was braced with a metal frame that formed a rigid structure from the tail panel to the bulkhead, and this was carpeted. With the engine cover in place, the whole installation was hidden

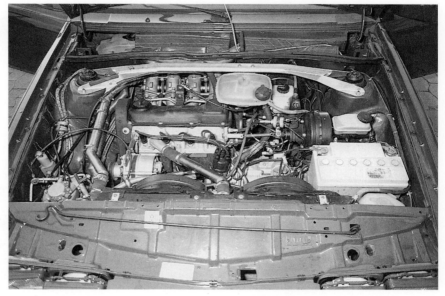

Twin-motor Scirocco was driven by journalists from Europe and America as well as by factory personnel. The engines had racing-spec fuel-injection systems and the body shell was heavily braced. The centre console, below, shows the doubling-up of all the vital gauges.

81

The second Bimotor Scirocco was evolved from the first prototype by the Development Department as a civilized road car that could have been produced in limited numbers.

from view.

The interior of the car was equally neat. Instead of a battery of supplementary gauges hogging the centre console as in the first prototype, a custom-made instrument panel had been assembled specially for the car by VDO who make all the instruments for VW. Fitting into the standard instrument pack hole, this contained a matching pair of rev counters with an LCD-readout speedometer in between. The bottom of each rev counter contained a small water temperature and oil temperature gauge, mirror imaged, and in the centre was the petrol gauge.

The underbonnet view was impressive. Now that the factory 1,781cc engine was in production, this early 1983 prototype was able to use the new block and coupled this to Oettinger 16-valve heads. This 1800E/16 engine gave 141bhp at 6,100rpm and 125lb/ft of torque at 5,500rpm. The fuel system was a modified Bosch K-Jetronic and the compression ratio was 10.2:1.

The surprise factor in this research vehicle was that the complex gear linkages connecting two five-speed manual gearboxes had been dispensed with in one fell swoop by using a pair of three-speed automatic gearboxes. The torque convertors were modified to optimize their response and the gearbox changeup points were adjusted to

suit the characteristics of the sporting Oettinger engines, and the whole set-up worked very well because the slight slip in the torque convertors would help to compensate when the two engines were running out of synchronization, as when the power balance between the front and rear engines was being modified.

Twin Golf

That same year, 1983, Kalle Grundel took the Group A Golf GTI rally car to victory in the German Rally Championship and, behind the scenes, VW Motorsport were starting work on its replacement as the new Golf was phased in. Up to that point, Group 1 and Group 1b GTIs had 148 or 150bhp for the track and the rally cars, in Group A, anything from 170bhp to 200bhp depending on spec. The Bimotor Scirocco was originally devised as a Group B rally weapon, but it was not until 1985 that the green light was given to incorporate the lessons learnt from this car into an official rally machine. The Twin Golf was not going to enter the fray of international rallying though; its objective was an attempt at the Pikes Peak hill climb record with successful GTI driver Jochi Kleint at the wheel.

Pikes Peak in the Rocky Mountains in Colorado is over 13,000ft high. The view from the

The gravel-surfaced Pikes Peak hill climb in the Rocky Mountains in Colorado provides a supreme test of competition vehicles, their design unhampered by any homologation requirements. The first twin-engined Golf driven at Pikes Peak by 1979 European Rally Champion Jochi Kleint had two 195bhp 1.8-litre power units. The second version, below, had turbocharging to overcome power loss at high altitude: despite a reduction in engine capacities to 1.3 litres each to keep the car in the same class, the total power output was up to 500bhp.

startline, over 8,500ft up, is breathtaking and of course the altitude extracts a heavy toll on naturally aspirated engines. The winding, loose-surface road up the mountain is 9.4 miles long and has 156 turns.

VW's challenge to nature had a pair of 1,807cc Oettinger engines of 195bhp apiece to power it and, running an 11.0:1 compression ratio, they supplemented the combined 390bhp at 7,500rpm with 338lb/ft of torque at 5,800rpm. Performance was not dissimilar to the Bimotor Sciroccos with a 0-60mph time of 4.3 seconds and a top speed of 162mph depending on final drive. It was quickly established that the altitude was doing the car's engines no favours and for a really serious assault on the Peak in 1986, a change of tactics was called for. To keep the car in its engine capacity class, and use turbocharging, VW had to resort to the use of much smaller engines. Their choice was the 1,300cc Polo engine, and these small power units were modified to take a KKK turbocharger each, with intercooling. Bosch K-Jetronic fuel injection was grafted onto the engines and boost pressure was variable between 1.4 and 2.0 bar. At peak boost, these 8.5:1 compression engines kicked out 250bhp each giving a sum total of 500bhp at 7,000rpm and 384lb/ft of torque at 6,000rpm. Weighing just 2,310lb, 100lb less than a Corrado and about 250lb heavier than a Golf GTI, the 1986 Twin Golf was good for a 3.4 second burst to 60mph and a top speed of 193mph!

That car was still essentially a Golf beneath the sheetmetal work, though, and for the 1987 attempt on the Peak, VW fielded what amounted to a silhouette racer. The centre section of the car was a monocoque cell constructed largely from aluminium in the best racing-car tradition. From this were hung the front and rear tubular space frames to which the engines and suspension components were attached. Although, to onlookers, the front and rear detachable engine covers were perfect replicas of a production Golf's, even with standard looking wheelarches, these were just glassfibre components held in place by quick release fixtures. The car weighed just 2,244lb and had 652bhp to propel it. That is a power-to-weight ratio of 3.43lb/bhp! Unlike all the previous cars, this one had the engines mounted in-line. Those engines were a pair of 1.8-litre 16-valve Golf engines prepared by Kaimann Racing to full competition spec. An intercooled KKK turbo-charger boosted each one to 1.3 bar at full throttle and, with the 8.5:1 compression ratio, output was

The last of the three Golfs for Pikes Peak was really a silhouette racer, with a pair of these 326bhp turbo engines specially prepared by Kaimann and longitudinally mounted.

652bhp at 6,800rpm and 428lb/ft at 6,400rpm. Two huge fans extracted air through the rear-mounted radiators giving the rear of the car the appearance of a James Bond movie car that looked equally capable of aquatic duties. 0-60mph took 4.1 seconds and the car was geared for just 114mph through Formula 2 Hewland gearboxes and running on 225/50VR16 tyres.

The three Pikes Peak Golfs never won their events but they finished in the top ten in the three years they competed. They provided valuable experience with regard to the synchronization of two engines in one chassis and what could be achieved with four-wheel drive. These full-house competition Twin Golfs were also the ultimate expression of an idea that was born over a few drinks in a bar seven years earlier.

VW Golf G60 Limited

In automobile production, economies of scale are all-important. The main Volkswagen plant is geared to produce cars like the Golf in runs extending ultimately to eight-figure numbers.

Inside the VW Motorsport workshops in Hannover, with three Rallye Golfs in various states of preparation.

The few hundred thousand Scirocco, Golf Cabriolet and Corrado models are farmed out to the coachbuilders Karmann. Even smaller runs like the 5,000 Rallye Golfs produced for motorsport homologation are made in the Brussels plant. One-offs or very small runs of really special cars are the speciality of VW Motorsport. For VW Motorsport is more than just the factory's competition department. Like BMW, VW sees its Motorsport division as playing a rather wider role. In their new premises in Hannover, VW Motorsport personnel are competition, development, limited edition production and customer special wishes rolled into one. They even have a restoration department which can turn rusting hulks into pristine exhibits for the VW AutoMuseum in Wolfsburg – or for customers.

In the squeaky-clean main workshops, a visitor would see the mechanics working on existing Rallye Golfs, or knocking new bodyshells into shape for their competition debut, while other specialists may even be building the 130bhp VW LT Van support vehicles that follow the rally cars to events. Turn the corner and you are confronted with the area where the 'specials' are built. A one-off heavily modified G60 Passat was being built for VW Motorsport head, Klaus-Peter Rosorius, during my visit, and in a bay next to it, a customer's standard looking Polo hatchback was in for servicing and tuning. It had a supercharged G40 engine under the bonnet; GTI performance in a shopping car! Directly opposite this a five-door Golf syncro with slightly flared arches and big wheels lay at rest. A turbocharged 200bhp 16-valve engine had been installed in this car.

The rest of the facility was given over to production of just 70 Limited Edition Golfs. Built

The Golf G60 Limited is a real wolf in sheep's clothing, its external appearance giving little clue to the 210bhp supercharged engine and four-wheel-drive running gear lurking beneath. One function of VW Motorsport is to undertake short production runs of special cars like this.

Engine of the Limited combines the 16-valve head and G-lader forced induction. VW Motorsport grille badge denotes the car's origin.

largely by hand, these cars were based on a five-door syncro with its viscous-coupled four-wheel-drive system. To this was added ABS, power steering, electric windows, central locking, steel sunroof, heated front seats, a full leather interior and an on-board computer.

Tuners in Germany have already begun to exploit the latent potential of the G60 engine, offering conversions ranging from 180bhp to 200bhp for the Corrado and Rallye Golf. VW Motorsport go one better right from the start by applying the G60 supercharger to the 16-valve rather than the eight-valve engine. The result is 210bhp (DIN) at 6,500rpm and 186lb/ft of torque at 5,000rpm with an 8.8:1 compression ratio and the supercharger providing 23psi of boost. More than that, this power is developed from an engine

with full compliance to US emission regulations via a pair of three-way catalytic convertors, a clean engine that runs on super unleaded fuel! Digifant electronic injection is important in achieving such controlled efficiency.

The Limited may look like a standard five-door Golf with 6½J x 15in BBS alloy wheels and 195/50VR15 Pirellis, but this wolf in sheep's clothing has the drivetrain from the Rallye Golf including its complete front-end beneath the standard front wings. This means that the inner arches are larger to take wide tyres without fouling the suspension and the new gearbox and large capacity radiator are also grafted in. Thus, various bits of the car are sent from Brussels and Wolfsburg to come together in Hannover. 210bhp in a car the size of a Golf is a lot, but the Limited is not a stripped-out racer; it is a compact, all-weather luxury express. It tips the scales at 2,805lb at the kerb which makes it some 700lb heavier than a GTI 16V. That weight eats into the performance, but even so 7.2-second 0-60mph time and a 142mph top speed is not to be scoffed at.

The Golf G60 Limited is the fastest production road car to have left any VW plant destined for a private customer. Like most of the projects that emanate from VW Motorsport, it was the brain-child of Klaus-Peter Rosorius. 'It took a long time to realise this project,' he explained, 'but we were fortunate to have the help of many engineers in the design and development department at Wolfsburg. The idea was to have a nice, elegant-looking production Golf without external modifications but lots of fascination under the bonnet.' That aim has been achieved by the 70 Limited cars which are restrained in outward appearance even to the point of having simple, single head-lamps. One customer who owns No 031 has fitted a four-lamp grille and wider 7J Borbet alloy wheels but all the other Limited cars have left the factory in their metallic anthracite paintwork with just the blue grille surround and subtle VW Motorsport badges to distinguish them as instant classics. As for the future, Limited Editions of the Corrado and Passat have not been ruled out and when the VW V6 engine is released, who knows what we might see from VW Motorsport.

6

The Karmann connection

No Volkswagen story would be complete without reference to the Osnabruck coachbuilders, Wilhelm Karmann GmbH. Over half a century older than VW itself, Karmann was founded in 1874 and taken over by Wilhelm Karmann on August 1, 1901. The company manufactured its first car bodies, for Dürkopp, Opel and Benz, the following year. The association with Volkswagen began in 1949 with production of the Cabriolet version of the Beetle, Type 15A. Eventually, Karmann made 330,000 of these cars and one of the very first now resides in the VW AutoMuseum in Wolfsburg. Karmann continued to produce specialized low-volume cars based on Beetle running gear for many years, introducing the famous VW Karmann Ghia coupe in 1955. That same year, Beetle production passed the magic 1,000,000 figure, an achievement never before recorded in German car-manufacturing history.

The entry of Volkswagen into the Brasilian market with a factory producing the Beetle and variants of it prompted Karmann to expand its own facilities and, in 1959, Karmann Ghia do Brasil was set up to meet VW's needs in that potentially huge market. The links between VW and Porsche helped Karmann gain business from the latter and they began to make some of the bodies for the 356B in 1961, beginning with the short-lived hardtop coupe version and then continuing with the standard coupe shape until the end of the 356 series. The 901 prototype was presented by Porsche at the Frankfurt Show in 1963, and when it went into production as the 911 and 912, Karmann were again able to provide Porsche with much-needed additional capacity, assembling and trimming bodies in parallel with Porsche's own Stuttgart plant. For the mid-engined 914, the joint VW-Porsche project launched in 1969, the bodyshells were all made by Karmann. In 1974, Karmann employees assembled the first of the new-generation VWs, the Scirocco.

A striking design study shown by Giugiaro at the Frankfurt Show in 1973 was a clean-cut coupe called Asso di Picche (Ace of Spades), interesting because it was based on the Audi 80 which shared its floorpan with the first Passat and provided the engine from which the GTI power unit was derived. Had this car been productionized, it would have been ahead of its time – and right in the Scirocco class. The Ace of Spades was built for Giugiaro by Karmann and now rests in the latter's museum.

Giugiaro and Karmann co-operated again, on officially VW-sanctioned Scirocco Mk2 prototypes in 1977. A wooden study was made first, with no interior, followed by a realistic metal mock-up. Both had the same overall shape, differing only in details like bumpers and lights. The wheelarch shapes, bumpers, and the crease in the flanks of the car echoed the Maserati Quattroporte prototype that Giugiaro showed at the Turin Motor Show the year before, under-lining how designers tend to use certain aesthetic motifs on more than one prototype before moving on. The wraparound bumpers and front indicator lights from the Scirocco II Study were adopted by VW on the production Mk1 for the 1978 model year showing how a completely different design proposal may influence a current model.

The most significant Volkswagen on the company's stand at the 1979 Geneva Motor Show

Study for a proposed Scirocco Mk1 replacement built by Karmann in 1977 to a Giugiaro design, with echoes of some of that studio's other designs of the period. This mock-up is now on display in the Karmann Museum.

A second shot at updating the Scirocco, also by Giugiaro, with a straight-through waist-line instead of the original's rising rear side-window line. Although neither of these proposals was taken up in its entirety, VW clearly took note.

Facelifted Scirocco for 1978: bumpers and front wings were revised, with front indicators wrapped around in the manner of the Giugiaro/Karmann proposal.

was the Golf Convertible. Just as the GTI started a new trend towards hot hatchback cars, the Golf Convertible was the first in a line of drop-top versions of modern front-wheel-drive cars. It was an entirely new species; cars like the Fiat 124 Sport Spyder or the Alfa Romeo Spider no doubt had the same mechanicals as their saloon and coupe brethren and, in the case of the Fiat, the same floorpan and suspension as well, but they were sporting two-seaters with little or no rear-seat accommodation. The Golf featured a modified hatchback bodyshell and thus retained the full four-seat capability of the original car. The prototype was produced by Karmann in 1976. The company was so well entrenched in producing Cabriolet Beetles and Karmann Ghias that it was a natural progression for them to build the first Golf Cabriolet for presentation to VW's Board, and undertake the subsequent production.

A variation on the same theme rolled out of the Osnabruck prototype shop a year after the Golf Cabriolet production line started rolling. The Jetta Cabriolet in some ways actually looked better proportioned than the Golf which had a high, stubby tail in production form. The Jetta never made it to production; the yellow prototype now sits in the Karmann Museum just sixty feet from the Golf Cabriolet study.

Karmann are coachbuilders rather than manu-

facturers. They may build prototypes of complete cars for manufacturers and indeed undertake the difficult transition from prototype to production for that manufacturer, but they still rely on their client for all mechanical assemblies. Thus the engine, gearbox, suspension and some interior components come from Volkswagen to be built into the Golf Cabriolets, Sciroccos and Corrados that roll out of the Karmann factories. Small-volume production is their speciality, and to give some idea of why Volkswagen sub-contracts the building of these models to Karmann, a comparison of Golf and Scirocco production figures is interesting. In 1988, VW in Wolfsburg announced that they had produced the 10 millionth Golf, 13 years after the launch of the first car. Between 1974 and 1981, Karmann produced 504,100 Scirocco Mk1s, and up to September 1989, they had made 272,000 Mk2 cars. From 1979 to September 1989, 267,000 Golf Convertibles were built. The first year of Corrado production totalled approximately 17,000 cars.

Coachbuilders like Karmann, however, do not always wait around to take their cue from major manufacturers like VW, Ford or BMW. With major resources at their disposal, it is today possible for them to build one-off prototypes or even just present their own interpretations of how they see a particular model evolving. The latter

Prototype Golf Cabrio now in the Karmann Museum. Note how slim its folded hood is compared with the elaborate double-layer production version. Karmann also made this Jetta Cabriolet, below: an attractive car, it was unfortunately too close to the Golf to warrant a limited production run.

Two of Karmann's envoys on the 1987 motor show circuit were this red Scirocco and subtly restyled white Golf Cabriolet.

case is more the norm and at major international motor shows, Karmann usually takes a stand not far from Volkswagen. Over the years, they have exhibited show cars with different spoilers, special paintwork, non-standard alloy wheels and invariably custom interiors in leather and fabric. A prime example is the red Scirocco 2 with colour-coded bumpers, Ronal alloy wheels and special half-leather interior that did the 1987 show circuit. The 1988 theme was a two-tone Scirocco and Golf Cabriolet pair, painted silver with metallic anthracite grey applied from bumper level down, extending to the wheelarches. 6J x 14in eight-spoke flat-faced alloy wheels from RH were used. The Scirocco 16V show car also had a colour-coded rear spoiler and wing mirrors, and had its rubber side protection strip removed. A different front grille with just three large horizontal slats was used. Inside, black leather with grey fabric inserts gave the cars a classy but still sporty feel.

The Frankfurt Show in 1989 was the first showing of a Karmann interpretation of the new Corrado, and the silver car that took pride of place on the revolving platform was tastefully and luxuriously appointed. The exterior was standard save for a set of attractive 7J x 15in Centra five-spoke alloy wheels which helped to fill out the arches and give the car a better stance. But the interior was upholstered in light tan and brown hide which complemented each other beautifully both in colour co-ordination and the way the two leathers were used to highlight facets of the car's interior sculpting. This is the sort of work that a coachbuilder like Karmann excels at and it would be a shame if VW missed the opportunity to commission limited runs of such cars.

Corrado prepared by Karmann and shown at the 1989 Frankfurt Show. 7J x 15in Centra alloy wheels and 195/50VR15 tyres fill out the arches.

The final stages of assembly at Karmann's Osnabruck plant. These Corrados will now be checked over, road tested and signed off for shipment to dealers all over the world.

7

Dream maker: Treser

Walter Treser is a leading supplier of aftermarket equipment for the Golf and Scirocco family. But he also deserves a special place of his own in this anthology of the GTI because, apart from Formula 3 racing cars, the Treser Sportscar is the only purpose-built special vehicle so far to use the Golf GTI powerplant. It was perhaps an obvious choice for someone who had worked at VW Audi before going independent. Along with Jorg Benzinger, Walter Treser shared joint parenthood of the Audi quattro concept. It was these two men who realised the potential of marrying the 4WD parts of the military VW Iltis to an Audi 80 saloon floorpan, and managed to convince the product strategy committee to approve the car for further development.

It had seemed that Walter Treser, the son of a hotelier, was destined to enter the world of gastronomy. As a boy, however, it was technology and cars in particular that became his fixation. He taught himself to drive at eight, built himself a motorcycle at 14 and by 18 had proved he could drive his car on two wheels. In 1962, aged 22, Treser passed his exams in automotive and aeronautical engineering and went to work for Daimler-Benz and then Veith Pirelli where he was put in charge of the experimental tyre department, developing low profile tyres like the P7. Treser moved to Audi in 1977 where he worked closely with Ferdinand Piech, head of the experimental department. It was not long before his obvious talent earned him the post of Head of the Preliminary Experimental Department and he became the youngest member of the Committee for Technological Strategy. With the development of the quattro under his belt, Treser under-

took the organisation of Audi's rally sport involvement. From March 1980 to August 1981, he was head of the Audi Competition Department. On January 1, 1982, Treser founded his own company, Walter Treser Automobiltechnik und Design in Ingolstadt to develop and manufacture high-quality aftermarket components for Audi cars as well as exclusive specialized models based on Audis. On August 26, 1985, he founded Walter Treser Automobilbau GmbH in Berlin to develop the sports car that had been his childhood dream.

An extremely high standard of design and manufacture enabled Treser to gain independent car manufacturer's status from the West German Federal Department of Transport soon after he started his business. Professionalism is something that he pursues relentlessly in his projects. Originality was another of his assets. Treser can never be accused of taking styling cues from other designers. He introduced blacked-out tail-lights on his quattros first. The factory subsequently adopted the style. His radical sculptured body-styling for Audi and VW cars has not been mimicked by anyone else.

There has been some debate as to whether the style of the Sportscar is the culmination of the design details that Treser had been working with in various Audi and VW styling kits up to that point or if indeed he was trying ideas for the Sportscar all along. The truth is probably a bit of both, but there is a clear lineage of development in his products, symbolized by a coloured drawing done for him by an employee and framed on his office wall. It shows an open door with the stylised '1' that is the Treser logo, in the distance. That '1' used to be an Audi corporate logo and Treser uses

Walter Treser, joint instigator of the Audi quattro programme, who went on to found his own tuning firm for Audi cars and then extended his expertise to the Golf GTI and Corrado.

Number one: the Treser logo reflects the unremittingly high standards which the organization sets itself.

it now with their authority, which shows the high regard they have for him.

Three prototypes and a few partly finished cars and several patents are lying around in the hands of the receiver, for sadly the Sportscar is no more, killed off by politics and short-sighted bankers who jointly and severally failed to see the up-and-coming international boom in the market for reasonably priced small sportscars. Those who refused to finance Treser in 1987 must now be kicking themselves in the wake of the success of cars like the Mazda MX5 Miata and Lotus Elan, the latter very similar in concept to Treser's ill-fated Sportscar.

In 1985, Treser's first company was doing a brisk trade. He had a staff of 65 and an annual turnover of £10 million. The time seemed right to embark on the Sportscar project. A well sorted styling and tuning programme, originally based around Audi cars, had been expanded to include the ubiquitous Golf GTI, beginning with alloy wheels, black tail-lights, gearknob and steering wheel. A new front grille and then a dramatic full body kit were added, followed by engine conver-

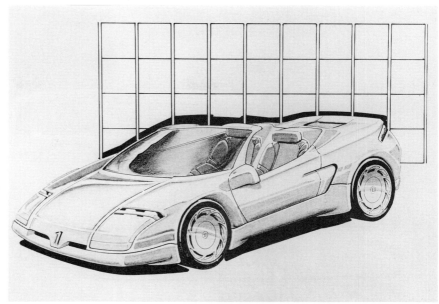

To build his own sports car was Treser's long-held dream: these early design sketches show many elements of style also seen in the components he produced for modifying Audi models.

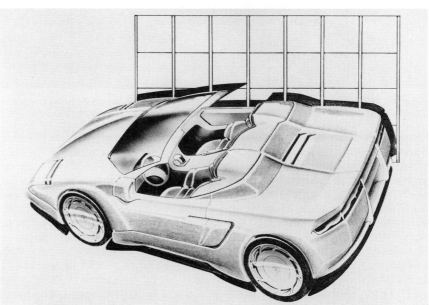

sions. The Sportscar required a compact and powerful engine that could be augmented by tuning parts already in the Treser programme. The logical choice was the VW GTI 16-valve unit, and the mid-engined two-seater was designed around this powerplant.

Designing, developing and manufacturing a whole new car is a very time-consuming and expensive business that must be measured in millions of Pounds, Dollars or indeed Deutsch-

marks. But Treser was initially lucky. He was given the first push away from the shore by the City of Berlin which was looking for dynamic young entrepreneurs. They delivered a factory site, a £500,000 research grant and various tax benefits to get the company going. But a larger Malaysian investor had pulled out of the project even before this, and raising the 15 million DM capital ultimately required was a hard uphill slog.

In the meantime, the Sportscar slowly took

What might have been. The GTI 16V-powered Treser Sportscar could have been a worthy rival to the new Lotus Elan, Toyota MR2 and Mazda MX5, and would have been able to use already available VW tuning parts.

shape. The first concept drawings existed as far back as autumn 1983. By May 1984 a wooden model had been made and wind-tunnel testing was underway. The first full-size model appeared in October 1985 and, in March the following year, the Treser stand at the Geneva Show had a full-scale half of the model mounted in a mirror wall to reflect the image of a complete car. A year later, the chassis prototypes were running, and the complete prototype was unveiled at the 1987 Frankfurt Show.

The little Sportscar was the centre of attraction on Treser's stand and the press information given away revealed that there was far more to the car than just a thoughtfully sculptured body based on VW Golf GTI 16V mechanicals. In his capacity as a recognized vehicle manufacturer, Treser was not content simply to sell a small number of cars to European countries. One of the serious export markets that Treser had found for his Audi conversions was the USA. The safety and emissions regulations there are complex and very trying for even large manufacturers, and require substantial financial investment for the testing and develop-

ment of components that comply. Treser was thus fortunate in being able to use the VW engine which was already certified for the USA should he decide to sell the car in that market.

While motive power was not a problem, the body structure and chassis had to be designed from the outset to comply with American DOT as well as European crash and safety regulations. Clumsy impact bumpers are a thing of the past thanks to new plastics technology used by manufacturers like Porsche, and to this end the Treser Sportscar was designed with a defined crash area filled with a foam material to absorb impact energy. The foam was embedded between the covering laminate shells of the deformable zone. Elastic front and rear bumpers were integrated and were designed to absorb parking bumps without damage.

Aerodynamically, a cigar-shaped vehicle is the theoretical ideal. In the real world this is impractical and so a Kamm tail is the next best thing. Although the two-seater Treser Sportscar is not a fastback in the true sense even when the top is raised, its profile resembles a wedged semi-

Distinctive Treser steering wheel is very comfortable, with thumb cut-outs to encourage the 'correct' quarter-to-three position of the hands.

Black tail lights and rear panel are a Treser notion which has caught on with GTI owners. This car also shows the Treser TRX wheels and tailgate with expensive replacement glass.

circle and gives smooth airflow over its contours, which have been sculptured in places as necessary to admit or extract air. The bodywork construction is novel. The body itself is glassfibre and Treser hold the patent for AVUS, a lightweight but very rigid aluminium composite structure which is used for the floor of the car. The material is corrosion resistant and easy to adapt to aerodynamic requirements. One of the aluminium chassis profiles is used as a service conduit and all the ducts and pipes required for cooling, brakes, clutch, gear selection and heat run through this. The front and rear suspensions are located on their own subframes. MacPherson struts are used at both ends with progressive minibloc springs, lower wishbones and anti-roll bars. Ventilated disc brakes are used at each corner.

Convertible cars are practical only when the sun is shining. The rest of the time the disadvantages – waterproofing, noise and security – are prominent. A detachable hardtop is a good solution but you cannot take it with you wherever

Treser grille effects as great a transformation of the Golf's frontal appearance as the tailgate does at the rear.

you go. The Treser Sportscar neatly sidesteps this problem with the design that Treser pioneered in 1983 on his quattro Roadster. An ingenious hinged hardtop with counterbalance weights disappears backwards below the rear deck when it is not needed and this solves the problem without impingeing on cabin or boot space.

When the first prototype was completed on March 29, 1987, optimism in the company was high and, despite mounting financial problems, Treser announced plans for a one-make race series using a slightly modified version of the car. The plan was that 30 cars, or about a week's production, would be committed to the series. The main championship sponsor was Hydro Aluminium, supplier of the alloy and plastic sandwich material used for the floor of the car, with co-sponsors Bilstein, Pirelli and Recaro. Just over a year later the Treser TR1 was able to give an impressive demonstration of its dynamic abilities in the first event of the planned series, held at the Avus track in Berlin. The race attracted 19 Treser owners from four countries, including Walter Treser himself. He started last on the grid and by the end of the race had worked his way up through the field to sixth position. It was a great tribute to Treser that all the cars finished the race, proving an important point about the thorough development and production-worthiness of the design. But fate took an unkind turn and a few weeks later the company was in serious trouble, with a possible last-ditch rescue attempt being negotiated with Oettinger. This fell through and

on August 16 the receivers were called in.

If there is a lesson to be learnt from Walter Treser's misfortune, it is that trying to design and build a car *and* raise finance at the same time is not humanly possible. Compared to what it would cost a major manufacturer to design, develop and tool up for a sportscar, the £5 million that Treser needed was peanuts; Mazda and Lotus have spent much more than that on the Miata and Elan. Once again, shortsighted financial institutions have totally misjudged the fast-moving motor industry and missed being able to back a company that would have been at the leading edge of the new wave of sportscar fever that has now gripped countries across the globe.

The originality of design and high-quality standards of manufacture that characterized the Sportscar are evident too in the products of the continuing Treser Audi and VW styling and tuning operation. Treser modifications for the GTI started off in 1984 simply as an extension of the bolt-on parts available for Audis. These first parts were the distinctive alloy wheels for the Golf and Jetta Mk2 cars made only in a metric size as Treser had an agreement with Michelin. This size is known as 165TR365 and is approximately 6½J x 14.4in. The tyre size is 200/55R365 TRX 86H – which makes our Imperial system seem simple by comparison! Also available were a Treser steering wheel and gearknob.

The next product was once again an extension of the work Treser had done on Audi cars. His black tail-light design had been picked up by Audi

Launched at the 1989 Frankfurt Show, the Treser Corrado styling kit has body modifications to complement the three-spoke wheels. Engine conversions range from a 210bhp G60 upgrade to a 240bhp turbocharged 16-valve unit.

for the upgraded quattro and Treser released a kit for the GTI which consisted of blacked tail-light covers and a black centre piece that attached to the tailgate. Visually, this helped to break up the bulk of the rear panel and proved very popular amongst GTI owners despite the high cost. The full body styling kit which followed in 1986 was very dramatic and completely changed the appearance of the Golf. It had to be laminated to the bodywork and was no weekend DIY job. Accompanying it was an optional new tailgate with a wraparound glass design. The special glass was very expensive to manufacture, and this was reflected in the price. Wider wheels and tyres became available with this kit and were once again the Treser/Michelin design but with 180TD390 (7.1J x 15.4in) rims and 220/45VR390 TRX tyres. Koni dampers and special springs were offered as a package to lower and stiffen the car.

By this time also, an engine modification package had been developed for the 16V and this involved reboring and fitting new pistons to bring the capacity out to 1.87 litres. The cylinder head was polished, ported and gas flowed and a new camshaft fitted which improved torque and economy. The result of these changes was 163bhp at 6,600rpm, up from 139bhp at 6,100rpm, but more significant was an improvement in torque throughout the range, taking out the dips in the standard car's curve, and peaking 12lb/ft higher at 5,000rpm.

Latterly, a simplified styling kit has also been offered which has a slightly different front grille, and you can buy the various parts individually. With the release of the Treser Corrado styling kit at the Frankfurt Show in 1989, Treser showed a new three-spoke alloy wheel design. This answered the criticisms of owners who did not wish to be restricted to the Michelin system. The wheel is available in 7J x 15in and 7J x 16in sizes for 205/50VR15 and 225/45VR16 rubber. Engine modifications that apply to the Corrado and Golf include a 240bhp turbocharged 16V engine or, for those with the G60, a useful power increase to 210bhp is achieved by modifications to the engine, supercharger and electronic fuel/ignition management.

8

Tuning for power and style

Amongst European languages, English and German share many root words. The old adage that there may be something lost in the translation also holds true, though, and one of the common words that has evolved a slightly different meaning in the two vocabularies is 'tuning'. On the British side of the Channel, 'tuning' means setting up correctly, as in the calibration of ignition and fuel settings to manufacturers' specifications. It can also refer to engine modifications for power. In German parlance however, 'tuning' takes on a broader meaning which covers other areas of vehicle modification. Thus, we have 'spoiler tuning', 'suspension tuning', and 'motor tuning'. Needless to say, people everywhere have been tuning cars for years to improve engine and chassis performance, but the commercial road-car tuner outside of the motorsport field is largely a phenomenon of the last three decades. The oldest of the VW tuners goes back further, though. Oettinger started off in 1946 with the Okrasa Beetle by fitting hydraulic brakes and then went on to extracting more performance from the flat-four engines.

Seven years later, Karl Meier, one of the first engineers with VW, designed the first spoiler for a road car. Enthusiasts quickly recognised the contribution this made to the stability of the Beetle at speed and his company, Kamei, grew from there.

Both BBS and Zender started around the same time, in 1970, the former making superlative light alloy wheels and the latter, spoilers. BBS was founded by Heinrich Baumgartner and Klaus Brand. The company name comes from their surname initials and that of Schiltach, the town the company is based in. They started off with the intention of making accessories for racing cars but before long this developed into the aftermarket for road cars too. The company was floated on the German stock exchange in 1987. Hans-Albert Zender started off as a one-man show and today employs over 300 skilled people in four linked companies that cover activities from design, marketing, original equipment manufacture and restoration to new car retail.

Another contemporary firm, D&W, also started in 1970. Detlef Sokowicz and Werner Bauer, an insurance salesman and a car accessories salesman respectively, were chatting in a pub in Dortmund about a business venture that would in time change the face of the aftermarket industry in Germany forever. They realized that the days of plastic roses and furry steering wheels were over and that quality and function were soon to be the industry watchwords. They withdrew their savings and opened a car accessories shop in Dortmund, carrying quality accessories from companies like BBS, Kamei and Zender. Their reputation soon spread far beyond the Ruhr and they were able to move to big new premises in nearby Bochum. The attraction for customers was a radical open-plan showroom where goods were imaginatively displayed. In the centre was a coffee bar with a selection of catalogues and motoring magazines for customers to browse through at their leisure while piped music provided a relaxed atmosphere. D&W has expanded dramatically with six of their own specialist stores in Germany and agents all over the world; nearly half a million of their specialist catalogues are sold every year and they have their own range of styling kits and accessories as well as continuing to sell the products of other manufacturers.

Campaign model GTI Mk1 for Continental markets had colour-coded wheelarch extensions and bumpers. Side stripes and P for Pirelli wheels were other features of this restrained factory venture into cosmetic tuning.

While body styling kits helped to differentiate one GTI from another, many of the fastest cars just had lowered suspension and wider wheels. This 2-litre Oettinger car is one such wolf in sheep's clothing, with an eight-valve 136bhp engine.

This GTI being driven in anger is wearing the first Zender body kit with front spoiler, larger wheelarches and sill extensions. The new grille looks striking in the mirror while four headlamps give better lighting. Alloy wheels are from BBS.

Further development of the Zender theme for the Mk1, with wider arches permanently integrated into the body finish rather than just screwed on, and modular wheels with separate rims.

The BBS styling kit of the era was softer and more rounded than the Zender offering. It was adopted by Oettinger for their converted cars and covered 205/60HR13 Pirelli P7 tyres on 6J x 13in ATS wheels.

The second Zender kit for the Mk1 was an over-bumper design that gave the car a more homogenous look. Note the subtle roof-top spoiler. This car was GTI Engineering's demonstrator in 1982. The alloy wheels were commissioned by Uniroyal to promote their 340 tyre range.

Zender also produced a more radical version of their kit with slightly squared-off arches for a more aggressive look.

Some owners just required better lighting and improved high-speed stability and might go for the Hella four-headlamp grille conversion and/or front spoiler with or without auxiliary lights, leaving the wheelarches as the factory provided them.

These big four German accessory manufacturers have been astute enough to spread their influence far and wide across the globe to America, Australia and Japan as well as most of the countries in between. But they would not have had the opportunity to do so were it not for the sudden craze for styling kits and wheels created by the phenomenal success of the Golf GTI. Before the Golf came along, only cars like the BMW 2002 and Opel Manta provided any sort of market for personalization. Mercedes-Benz made superb but rather staid cars which did not appeal to the younger buyers. The Golf on the other hand had the perfect image to scoop up buyers from all age groups and all walks of life.

Kamei, BBS and Zender all responded to the new VW with front and rear spoilers and then complete body kits. Before long, many other smaller companies jumped on the bandwagon and were creating their own designs to offer customers even more variety. Most of these kits started off being made from glassfibre, but, as production numbers increased, the bigger firms started to use more exotic materials like polyurethane and PU-RRIM which are injection moulded and less easily damaged in daily use. But the tooling for such mouldings is very expensive, so the smaller companies still use hand-laid glassfibre today.

The early designs were very functional; they were meant to enhance the shape of the car by offering a more integrated look, enhance aerodynamics by incorporating a front spoiler with brake cooling ducts and enhance the stance and roadholding by offering the chance to cover wider wheels and tyres. As time went by, more radical changes were made by designers like Michael Neumann of Style Auto, who created a very sculptural styling kit for the Golf. The more brutal lines of the Zastrow kit appealed to others, while in Italy, Orciari sought to change the frontal appearance of the car dramatically. Engine cooling was not one of this kit's strong points! Further down the line, Walter Treser was the first to undertake a serious styling change to the Golf 2 that looked integrated rather than stuck on, but the prohibitive cost of his kit precluded a flood of sales.

In the meantime, Vittorio Strosek had created the sensational wide-bodied Ferrari and Mercedes for Koenig, and this style, introduced at great expense to the top end of the market, began to filter its way down to the GTI enthusiasts. Thus, the late 1980s found a rash of wide-body kits on sale for the Golf and Scirocco. Notable ones come from Rieger Tuning who has the widest range of kits with small and intermediate body size alternatives on a similar theme. While the small BBS and Zender style kits can be painted and fitted by a skilful DIY enthusiast, the wide-bodied kits require the full facilities of a body shop and take as long as three weeks to fit properly. They need the cutting away of the original wheelarches, bonding, laminating and foam filling. The need then to virtually respray the whole car has given many people the excuse to make the colour change they always fancied.

European styling kits soon found their way across the Atlantic. This VW Rabbit which was APS's demonstrator in the early 1980s is wearing a Kamei kit and BBS wheels. Hidden from view are Bilstein suspension and a 2-litre 16-valve 170bhp Oettinger engine.

The most radical styling kit in the early 1980s was the Kamei X1. You either liked it or you didn't . . .

The Jetta, with its capacious boot, was a popular small saloon in the USA. It was included in the styling kit boom, too. This car prepared by APS was fitted with a BBS kit and three-piece BBS alloy wheels.

Integrating the bumpers with a styling kit could be done fairly subtly, as in the Zender design, or made to grab attention as this Zastrow effort does.

Early Golf styling kits were not left entirely to the Germans. A British-made kit which enjoyed some success was this design from Cartel.

The Kamei kit for the Scirocco Mk1 could be left in black or painted to match the body. This was another project car from APS in California. The wheels are by Exim.

A well known Scirocco in Britain was the Storm modified for noted author and motoring writer Leonard Setright. It had a blueprinted GTI Engineering 1600 Plus engine, Bilstein Sportpak suspension, 7J x 15in ATS wheels with 205/50VR15 Pirelli P700 tyres and a Zender body kit. The car was subsequently acquired by this writer.

The smartest early Scirocco in the USA was surely this 1981 car modified by Californian Bruce Berkey. Parts from various Kamei kits produced a unique look. Wheels are 7J x 15in Momo Pulsars.

When the Golf Mk2 came out, body and suspension kits were not immediately available, as the engine was very similar to that of the Mk1, hot but discreet GTIs with lowered suspension and bigger wheels were the rage in early 1984. This colour-coded car from Dennert Motorsport was typical of the breed.

Connaught Design did this GTI for Alpine Electronics UK Ltd in 1987: the retrimmed interior is subtle and tasteful, complementing the outward appearance.

Until the advent of the wide-body trend, most styling kits for the Golf Mk2 were variations on a theme, with front and rear spoiler and valance sections either integrating with existing bumpers, covering them or replacing them. Here is a selection of cars from: ASS Autosport . . .

Bubble Car of Italy . . .

BBS, sold through UK VW
dealers . . .

Foha, based in Austria . . .

Abt Tuning . . .

Kat, with turbo decal . . .

Hella, with four of their rectangular headlamps . . .

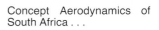

Concept Aerodynamics of
South Africa . . .

Concept again, on a 1986
GTi owned by VW of South
Africa . . .

AutoTech of California . . .

Kamei, comparing their kits
for the Mk1 and Mk2 . . .

and the Zender 90 kit.

Bridging the gap between British and American GTI tuning was this Steiner Engineering Golf with Auto-Tech body kit and 160bhp supercharged engine.

All this aftermarket activity did not go unnoticed by VW, as witness this 'design study' for the GTI 16V: production versions
were very close to this specification.

Whatever the tuners could do, the factory could do as well
or, often, better when they chose to. Just 70 metallic black
Golf Limited cars were made by VW Motorsport in 1990
and sold for the equivalent of £21,000 in Germany in left-
hand-drive form only. Combining the G60 supercharger
and 16-valve engine with syncro four-wheel-drive, all
within a very restrained outward appearance, this was the
ultimate hot hatchback.

Neat and functional external modifications do little to advertise the fact that this Abt Tuning Golf has a 220bhp turbocharged 16-valve engine. With that sort of power on tap it is just as well that it also has the syncro four-wheel-drive system.

Another relatively undemonstrative car is this one from Callaway, the first US tuner to turbocharge the Golf successfully, with an intercooled system that could produce up to 186bhp.

Most of what applied to the Golf could also be applied to the Jetta. This is a Zender kit applied to a limited edition of 50 cars put together by GTI Engineering.

The Zender kit for the Jetta again, used for a 16-valve Executive tuned by Steve's Auto Clinic in South Africa.

This is a Hella kit on a US-specification Jetta GLi from APS in California.

Proving the point that the Golf is the most modified of the hot VWs by far is the limited number of kits available for the Scirocco. This Zender front spoiler helped to clean up the aerodynamics and give a more ground-hugging look to the author's Scirocco GTi. The car also had Koni sports suspension, BBS 6J x 15in wheels with 195/50VR15 BF Goodrich Comp T/A tyres, and 125bhp from a camshaft and manifold conversion.

This full body kit is available from BBS (with the blessing of VAG (UK) Ltd) for those who want a more radical change in appearance.

The factory had their own ideas about how to cover very wide rubber. This car belonged to the experimental department in 1982 and was used for engine and suspension testing.

Volkswagen were more liberal with the slower-selling Scirocco when it came to fitting body styling modications to enhance showroom appeal. The Kamei kit was chosen for the 1983 GTX model in Europe.

Kamei's own interpretation of the Mk2 Scirocco included different wheels and some additional body details. Note also the absence of the side bump strip.

Some VW dealers in Britain created their own limited editions. Newbourne Garages of Croydon did this 'NGL Special' with a Kamei kit, Zender rear spoiler and BBS wheels.

In 1984 VAG (UK) Ltd commissioned a Mk2 Scirocco Storm. It had a body kit produced for VW by Zender but not made available in the aftermarket. The wheels were a new pattern from VW Design.

For 1988, the specially made Zender kit was used to create the Scirocco Scala, no longer confined to the UK market.

The entire Scala body was finished in matching paint, and the colour coding extended to the interior and the non-polished areas of the alloy wheels.

The Cabriolet came in for its share of aftermarket treatment too. This car seen at a Golf Cabriolet Club meeting in Germany has wider wheels and lowered suspension as well as a distinctive paint job.

This 1988 Scirocco study by Karmann with special two-tone paint and interior in matching hide shows how elegant the model could look.

Another of Karmann's products, the Golf Cabriolet, benefits from a similarly stylish treatment.

A body-coloured lip on the edge of the bonnet lowers the apparent grille height on this large-wheeled Cabriolet prepared by Nothelle.

Kamei produced this Golf Mk2-based Speedster in 1984. Despite the appeal of this design, there will be no open Golf from VW on a new floorpan until the arrival of the third-generation car expected in 1992.

One of the simplest ways of giving the car a distinctive look has always been reworking the grille design, perhaps with the aim, conscious or otherwise, of gaining more 'overtaking presence' when seen in the rear-view mirror. This Oettinger four-headlamp conversion using Hella DE lights is a straightforward example.

More ferocious looking is this Autoshop Hartmann conversion with a new bonnet, four-headlamp grille and Hofele Design bumper unit which uses Audi-style indicators and fog lamps.

Abt Tuning quattro Sport kit gives the Golf a facial resemblance to its 306bhp 4WD distant cousin from the Audi stable. Some turbocharged Abt cars have over 200bhp, so they are not all show and no go.

Retaining the standard grille is this GFL Sportline conversion. This is the over-bumper style of body kit which is the final stage before the wide-body kits which involve major reworking.

If four headlamps are not enough, you can always have six! This D&W grille would fit an otherwise standard car but is here fitted to a wide-bodied Golf with Rieger Tuning kit bodywork. The BBS wheels have 8in and 11in rim widths.

Perhaps the most radical face change for a Golf is provided by the venetian blind front of the Italian Orciari kit. The headlamp cover slats rotate when the lights are switched on.

Newest addition to the hot VW family is the Corrado, as accomplished a piece of design as you could wish for. The traditional grille front, rather than the more obviously aerodynamic Passat style, was felt to be in keeping with the model's sports car image.

New though it may be, the Corrado has already come in for some serious attention from the tuners. This RSS Design Corrado bears the hallmark of a company which has produced some radical front-ends for Golfs and Sciroccos.

Nothelle install a four-headlamp grille on the Corrado and fit their distinctive 16in wheels the pattern of which is derived from three 'n' motifs linked by a solid triangle. The G60 engine is uprated to 185bhp.

Putting a more aerodynamic front on the Corrado is this Projektzwo conversion for grille, front and rear valances and wheels.

Kamei replace the front and rear one-piece factory bumper/spoiler panels and add matching side skirts. Top box is optional for skiers!

The Zender styling kit is the most radical bolt-on conversion and can be used with wheels up to 8J x 15in dimensions.

Under its Zender-modified bodywork this Corrado prepared by BR Motorsport and Eurostyling packs a 190bhp 2-litre 16-valve engine.

The Corrado which Karmann exhibited at the 1989 Frankfurt Show featured this stylish interior in two-tone hide.

Beyond the realm of bolt-on body kits and with wheels wider, in the case of the Golf, than seven inches, modifications to the existing panels begin to be the order of the day. The rounded wheelarch style is typified by this car from Folger . . .

this one from Zender . . .

and two cars with unidentified conversions, photographed at the GTI Treffen in Austria.

Wheelarches flared in the manner of the Audi quattro are a more aerodynamic solution. This Oettinger car neatly covers its 8J x 15in wheels this way and at a quick glance looks like the factory Rallye Golf. The rear view is equally purposeful looking, with a badge revealing its 2-litre fuel-injected 16V power unit.

This is the factory version, one of 5,000 Rallye Golf G60s built to secure the motorsport homologation of the supercharged car with arches wide enough to accommodate the tyres needed for effective competition use.

Two more cars seen at the GTI Treffen, both copying the quattro style and looking similar at a glance . . .

but revealing many detail differences in the arches and side skirts.

Arches in a more square style, trying perhaps to echo the chiselled shapes of the basic Golf, are a feature of this car, based on an Italian Orciari kit.

Dramatic and rare. This Treser GTI (left and opposite) is the only one of its kind in Britain. Front, side and rearward aspects of the car are all changed by this comprehensive kit.

Offering another interpretation of the flared side panel look, this time on the Mk1 Golf, the Style Auto kit is a real head-turner.

This Folger version is different again, relatively restrained on the Mk2 . . .

but more radical and heavy-handed on the Mk1 Golf.

A much more subtle wide-flared design is the Z600 from Zender.

After the wide flares come the *really* wide-bodied cars on which much larger rear wheels are used. This WS Golf has a 170bhp engine by Wendland Motorsport and a white leather interior. The 15in diameter BBS wheels are 8in and 11in wide, with 225/50VR15 and 285/40VR15 tyres.

While the Germans have started doing wide wheelarch extensions on the Scirocco only in the last six or seven years, this car was converted in Britain by Autocavan as far back as the late 1970s.

A good example of the wide-body trend is this Rieger Tuning Scirocco GTO, based on the Mk1 car.

Rear view of the Rieger Scirocco emphasizes the ground-hugging, competition car look.

Under the bonnet of the Rieger car is a 16-valve engine. Note also the brace between the strut tops.

Widest of the wide! This Zander Exclusiv Scirocco has 8J and 13J BBS wheels with 225/50VR15 and 345/35VR15 tyres.

Interior of the Zander Scirocco has been totally reworked in dramatic style.

Of all the VWs, the Scirocco Mk2 is arguably the shape that takes wide-body styling best. It is a long and low car that can look stunning with a kit like this one from Rieger.

Scirocco from Kerscher has distinct Ferrari overtones as well as a name with sports-racing connotations.

This version of the wide-body Scirocco theme is from WS Styling.

Another shark-like conversion is this crisp and beautifully integrated Scirocco Z600 from Zender. There is no doubt that cars like these turn heads more than your average Porsche.

The most radical Scirocco of them all, from VW themselves, was the twin-engined car produced by the Motorsport and Development teams. Positively restrained in appearance compared with some of the independent tuners' efforts, it was the only one that really *needed* air vents at the rear. As competent on the race circuit as on loose surfaces, it was finished to road-car standards.

Inevitably, the wide-body look has got to the Corrado as well. With its gills, slats and scoops, this Rieger Tuning conversion adds drama to the sleek lines of VW's flagship coupe.

While the body-kit approach to tuning tends to be extrovert and attention-seeking, it was the obverse of the GTI's nature, its Q-car aspect, the performance car in a plain wrapper, that appealed to many. For some, though, even a 180bhp turbo conversion was not enough. Gunter Artz in Hannover split a Golf body-shell and widened it to cover Porsche 928 mechanicals. Only the doors and sidepanels are Golf, everything else had to be fabricated. The windscreen alone cost £2,000, so this was not a cheap exercise.

Less subtle is this Sbarro creation called the Golf 300S which is a front-engined, rear-wheel-drive car powered by a 928S V8 engine. The designation refers to the 300bhp power output.

There have never been estate car versions of the Golf or Jetta from the factory, but the Swiss company Uffler produced this six-wheeled heavy-duty estate – or is it a hearse?

The coupes too have been turned into carry-alls: Artz was responsible for this 'Sciwago'. Nordstadt are VW dealers who have boldly commissioned a number of these special projects (back when the Beetle was current, they did a mid-engined Porsche 914-based 1303).

A more recent coupe-estate is based on the Corrado and was produced by Chris Hahn of Design+Technik in Hamburg.

VW's own Golf-based commercial, the Caddy pick-up, is another ideal basis for the custom builder's art: this stylish yet still practical variation on the Caddy Sport theme had Zender styling and a 1.8-litre injection engine.

A project initiated by VAG (UK) Ltd, this Golf Caddy Sport was developed in 1985 to emphasize the leisure aspect of the versatile pick-up. A body kit and wheels by BBS, and support rails for a windsurfing board were the visible changes, while a GTI engine lurked under the bonnet.

Another exercise to combine GTI performance with a specialized practical utility was VW's own off-road 4x4 project, called Montana at its first appearance in 1989 and later renamed Country. Much-raised suspension and syncro transmission made it a workable proposition, not just a showpiece.

One manifestation of the desire among some of the German tuners to be different at all costs is the practice of changing the door hinging arrangements. Zander offered a Countach-style forward-tipping design for the Mk1 Scirocco, as well as a gull-wing conversion both for that car and for the Golf Mk2.

Dissatisfied with the standard Golf interior, some tuners graft in the dashboard from a more expensive car. Car Noblesse set upon this standard-looking Cabriolet and installed a cream leather-covered Porsche 911 interior with four matching Recaro seats.

SCS produced this Targa-topped GTI for those who want something between a saloon and a Cabriolet.

The interior of the SCS car features the dashboard from a 3-series BMW but with a special digital instrument pack.

Back in 1984, b&b were ahead of their time with this radically restyled Golf.

For those without the budget for a real Golf Cabriolet, the Ostermann conversion for a hatchback might be the answer. The hood folds flat, giving better rearward visibility than the Karmann version, and the car has a much larger boot, too.

Inside the Ostermann convertible can be seen the structural reinforcement added within the perimeter of the cabin, a simple and rugged engineering solution.

Soon after the Corrado was launched, convertible versions were announced by two after-market tuners, this version coming from Zender.

A much more radical approach to sporting, open-air, GTI-powered motoring was the Treser Sportscar with its advanced-technology composite structure. The mid-engined configuration was a no-compromise design for optimum handling and roadholding, at the expense of any '+2' seating.

Wheels and tyres

Both in visual terms and for the sake of handling and roadholding, the first move you should make when tuning your car is in the wheels and tyres department. A nice set of alloy wheels with low-profile tyres really sets a car off even before you get involved in uprated suspension and body styling. The difference is instantly visible when you compare the car to a standard one of the same type, and the low-profile rubber gives you better handling, grip and braking, making your car safer as well as more satisfying to drive.

The larger the wheel, the lower the profile the tyre needs to be to maintain the same gearing and rolling radius (important for speedometer calibration). A larger wheel looks better and helps to fill out the wheelarches visually. It also exposes the brakes to better airflow and thereby aids brake cooling when the car is being driven hard. For early cars which came on 5½J x 13in wheels, the natural upgrade was the so-called Plus One conversion. Using 185/60HR14 tyres on 6J x 14in wheels, this provided the same rolling radius as the 175/70HR13 standard rubber but put more rubber on the ground. The Plus Two system was

195/50VR15 rubber on 6J x 15in alloys. This was the largest size that could be accommodated under standard arches. The use of this tyre size with 7J x 15in alloys is possible, but on some cars the wheelarches have to be radiused or contact will be experienced over big bumps or when the car is loaded.

The very latest trend is to 16in diameter wheels as with the Nothelle package for the Golf Rallye, but only a car with as much wheelarch clearance as the Rallye can use these wheels without arch modification. The tyre size in 205/45VR16. When going to such wheel sizes, always bear in mind that the larger the wheel and the lower profile the tyre, the greater the chance of wheel damage on rough roads. Large potholes have been known to bend expensive alloy wheels, so if you live in an area with badly made roads, both ride comfort and your wallet may dictate no more than a Plus One wheel and tyre package. Also, when you are considering putting more rubber on the road, remember the law of diminishing returns. A 20% increase in tyre width gives you a 10% increase in grip – but only up to a certain point. Complications like over-sensitivity to

Replacement wheels and tyres can dramatically improve both the looks and the handling of a car, and they should be your first step in modification. This 171bhp Oettinger GTI 16V is wearing 7J x 15in BBS three-piece wheels and Pirelli P7 195/50VR15 rubber.

The wide-arched Golf Rallye G60 benefits visually and in terms of grip from the Nothelle 7J x 16in wheels and 205/45ZR16 Bridgestone tyres. Filling out the arches of any car gives it a more purposeful look.

changes in road surface such as patches and white lines, and a sharp deterioration in grip and steering feel under difficult conditions – when there is standing water on the road, for example – can set in if you pursue the wide tyre philosophy too far.

Suspension tuning

Following wheels and tyres, the next priorities in modifying your car to make it perform better are suspension and brakes, again before you touch the engine. You will find that with more cornering power at your disposal, your point-to-point times will be quicker anyway, as cornering speeds will begin to be limited only by visibility, by the need to retain the vital ability to stop safely within the distance you can see to be clear.

You will also find that a car with better suspension control is more comfortable to ride in as it does not roll so much in corners or give that uncomfortable wallowing sensation when driving on bumpy roads. Again, you can go too far. A car that is made too stiff in its suspension settings can be most uncomfortable. It is jiggly, you can leave the seat over big bumps and you will have less traction in bumpy corners as the car takes off over undulations. And it is skittish in the wet.

Ride and handling are thus a compromise, and VW in fact set a very high standard with the stock fuel-injected cars. The Mk1 cars are slightly underdamped and prone to rock-roll slightly in fast bumpy bends but the Mk2 car is superb straight out of the box. That is not to say that the Mk2 GTI cannot be improved. Far from it. To understand fully how the various suspension tweaks improve a car's handling, let us look at the

forces acting on a car when it is driven on the road or track.

Roll: a by-product of cornering, roll takes place along the longitudinal axis and in a softly sprung vehicle tries to lean the car excessively to the detriment of comfort and cornering ability. The more a car rolls, the greater the slip angles of the tyres and the less of the useful tread area is doing work. The primary component that will reduce this condition is the anti-roll bar, or swaybar as it is called in America.

Pitch: occurs on the transverse rotational axis and causes a car to dive under braking or squat under acceleration. In the absence of anti-dive, anti-squat geometry being designed into the suspension by angling the lower arm locating points, the springs and dampers play the major role in reducing the amount of pitch. Good progressive suspension prevents harsh oscillations.

Yaw: a force that provokes body motion around the vertical axis, yaw affects all the suspension components. In an ideal situation, a vehicle's suspension should provide completely neutral handling, but most cars are designed to provide mild understeer which allows the front of the car to go wide in corners. This is a safe characteristic to keep the average driver from getting into trouble especially when braking or suddenly decelerating in a bend where a neutral vehicle could then move into oversteer and perhaps spin. If you stiffen just one end of the car at a time, you can induce severe yaw conditions; stiffening the rear induces oversteer while stiffening the front

146

When driven on road or track, a car is subject to varying forces which try to rotate it around the three major axes, causing roll, pitch and yaw.

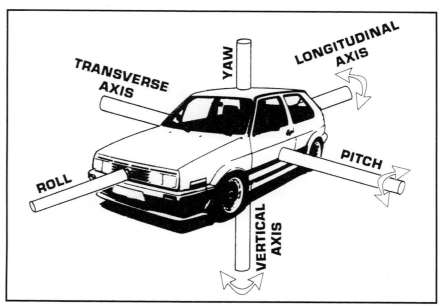

only creates understeer. Suspension development is very much a question of balance.

Modifications: to save customers a lot of time and trouble, aftermarket suspension manufacturers have developed kits for various cars providing just uprated springs, or dampers, or matching springs and dampers (which is better), as well as upgraded anti-roll bar kits to be used with the stock suspension or in conjunction with the spring and damper kits. The European manufacturers, like Bilstein, Koni, Sachs, Spax and others, favour the spring and damper kit approach while the Americans, with a more conversion-orientated custom-car background, tend to go the whole hog with upgraded anti-roll bar kits and better quality locating bushes as well.

Bushes locate suspension components to prevent metal-to-metal contact and provide isolation from road shock and noise. They are used in all moving components in the suspension and steering in modern cars and if a manufacturer

is over-generous with these rubber bushes, the car can feel rubbery in its handling and ride. Too much lateral movement in suspension bushes does not help accurate suspension location and makes a car feel woolly in corners. Conversely, the metal or metal and nylon rose joints used in racing suspension are too hard and direct for road use and would destroy themselves in short order. Upgraded high-quality road-car bushes made of polyurethane, like the AutoTech ones, will keep the suspension components in check while maintaining adequate comfort. Polyurethane steering bushes will sharpen up the GTI's steering, which has a slightly dead feel about the straight-ahead position.

AutoTech in California are US distributors for Hor Technologie parts. Hor are an original-equipment manufacturer who supply suspension, exhaust and other components to German car makers like BMW and VAG but who do their own range of aftermarket parts too. AutoTech are also agents for the excellent Japanese-made Tokico

AutoTech's polyurethane steering bushes tauten steering response and stop the rack moving horizontally in its mountings.

147

More polyurethane bushes. From left to right these are for the Golf/Jetta Mk2 lower front suspension arms; rear shock absorber top mounts; 15mm front anti-roll bar (standard GTI size); and 18mm front anti-roll bar (Jetta and Corrado).

Adjustable dampers are available in Europe from Spax and Koni. With the Dutch-made Koni set, shown here, the rear spring-pan height is also adjustable. Note the progressive-rate coil springs.

adjustable shock absorbers which match up well with Hor springs. The UK agents are Steiner Engineering.

Amongst the European suspension manufacturers, you will find that each of the kits you can buy has different characteristics and so will please customers looking for different kinds of performance. The Koni suspension has adjustability of damper settings as its strength. You can raise and lower the rear spring pans to adjust ride height and the dampers can be tailored from soft to fairly hard settings if you want to commute in

First on the scene as a complete suspension set was the famous Bilstein Sportpak.

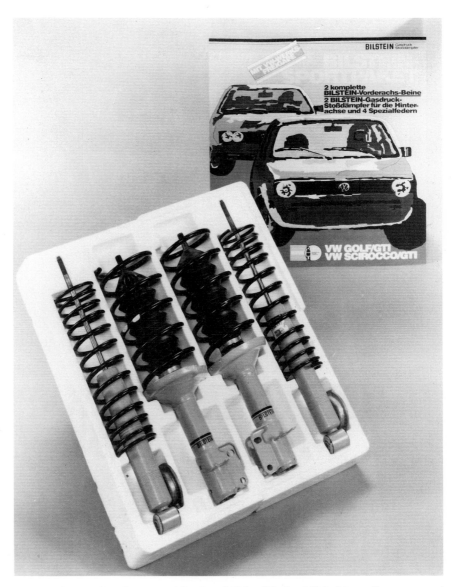

the week and then do club events at the weekend. Koni now have another damper design with a semi-active electronically controlled system – the normal kit is user-adjustable from the shock towers.

The Bilstein Sportpak was the first kit on the market for the original GTI and gives a firm ride but brilliant handling. It may be too firm for those who live near less-than-smooth roads, and the gas filled dampers are not adjustable. The kit for the Mk2 is more supple and was the last of the three Europeans to appear.

While Sachs were last on the scene with the Mk1 GTI kit, they were at the head of the queue

with the Mk2. Their Mk1 kit strikes a good comfort/handling balance for most people but may still be too soft for really press-on drivers. The Sachs Mk2 kit, on the other hand, is well-nigh perfect, with very little comfort lost over the standard suspension, and it also gives very progressive handling on the limit. All these kits lower the ride height by about an inch which helps stability.

It is not unusual for road testers in different countries to form slightly different opinions of a given car, especially in ride and handling terms. There are several reasons for this, not least of which is that suspension settings are in fact often

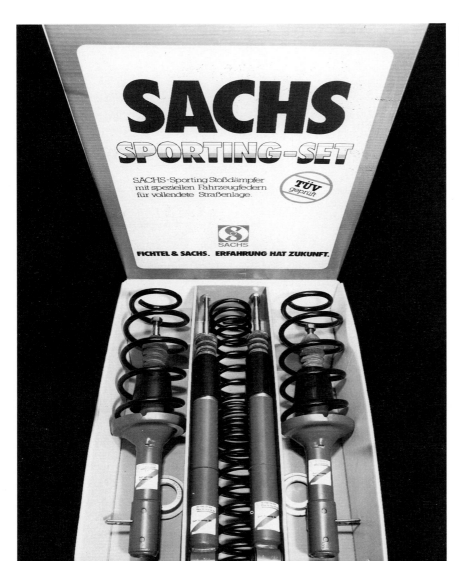

Of the three kits for the Mk1 cars, the Sachs offers the best ride quality but may be too soft for heavy-duty work.

tailored to the country of destination. The Americans like a softer-riding car despite the good quality of their roads and enthusiasts then complain that the car does not handle properly. Grip and tyre noise are affected by the content of the road surface and this varies from country to country. Thus, a Pirelli P6 manufactured in the UK for local use may turn out to be different from one made at Pirelli's German factory or indeed one made in the home market of Italy. Suspension, wheel and tyre tuning must thus be done for local conditions and, on that score, companies like

Automotive Performance Systems (APS) in California specify different damper settings for their Bilstein kits from those that you would find in Europe. By the same token, a German-bought set might prove a touch hard for use in the UK. Caveat emptor...

Anti-roll bars: the suspension design of the Golf and Golf-derived cars allows the inside rear wheel to pick up under hard cornering. While this is safe in practice, it is indicative of a very severe roll attitude. The solution is to increase the roll

SUSPENSION RECOMMENDATIONS

Through our research and development of chassis systems, we have arrived at what we think is the best combination for each type of vehicle. Please understand that these are only recommended combinations. They are a good place to start for those uninitiated with suspension modifications. We invite you to SportTune your own vehicle for its particular needs and your driving requirements. Our technical department will be glad to assist you with any special requests or problems.

Rabbit/Scirocco/Jetta 1:

Swaybars - 19mm front with a 25mm rear
HÖR Technologie Progressive Spring Set
Tokico Illumina Shocks or Bilstein HD Shock Absorbers
Stressbars: upper front, lower front (subframe), and rear.
(Note: Going too large on the swaybar size can make the car unmanageable in undulating terrain or on wet roads.)

Scirocco 16V:

Swaybars - 22mm front with a 28mm rear (upgrade from standard sizes)
HÖR Technologie Progressive Spring Set
Tokico Illumina Shocks or Bilstein HD Shock Absorbers
Stressbars: upper front and rear.

Cabriolet:

Swaybars - 22mm front with a 28mm rear
HÖR Technologie Progressive Spring Set
Tokico Illumina Shocks or Bilstein HD Shock Absorbers
Stressbars: upper front, lower front (subframe), and rear.
(Due to the "top-heavy" nature of this chassis, we recommend an upgrade in bar size over that of the standard Rabbit chassis.)

Golf/Jetta 2:

Swaybars - 22mm front with a 28mm rear
HÖR Technologie Progressive Spring Set
Tokico Illumina Shocks or Bilstein HD Shock Absorbers
Stressbars: upper front and rear.

Golf GTi/Jetta 2 GLi:

Swaybars - 22mm front with a 25mm rear (rear sizing due to integral torsion/swaybar on rear suspension)
HÖR Technologie Progressive Spring Set
Tokico Illumina Shocks or Bilstein HD Shock Absorbers
Stressbars: upper front and rear.

Golf and Jetta 16V:

Swaybars - 22mm front with a 25mm rear (rear sizing due to integral torsion/swaybar on rear suspension)
HÖR Technologie Progressive Spring Set
Tokico Illumina Shocks or Bilstein HD Shock Absorbers
Stressbars: upper front and rear.

Corrado:

Swaybars - 22mm front with a 25mm rear (rear sizing due to integral torsion/swaybar on rear suspension)
HÖR Technologie Progressive Spring Set
Tokico Illumina Shocks or Bilstein HD Shock Absorbers
Stressbars: upper front and rear.

SHOCK ABSORBER CHART

Shocks play a critical role in a vehicle's handling and are the most susceptible to wear. The lines we carry; Tokico, Sachs, and Bilstein, are gas pressurized to improve handling and comfort. To dispell anything you may have commonly believed about shocks, your shocks are not shock absorbers at all, but suspension dampeners. Their actual function is to dampen the oscillations of the springs created when the vehicle is in motion.

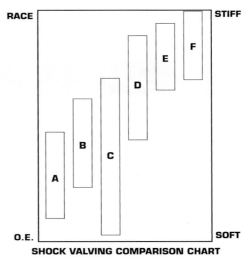

SHOCK VALVING COMPARISON CHART

The above chart illustrates the difference in shock absorber valving from one manufacturer's settings to another on the shocks we offer. This comparison is general, but should aid in the selection of shocks for your vehicle.

A - Sachs Super/Bilstein HD
B - Tokico HP (non-adjustable)
C - Tokico Illumina range of adjustment
D - Bilstein Sport
E - Bilstein Rallye/Race
F - Bilstein Race (also Group 2 race)

Guide to suspension tuning reproduced with the kind permission of AutoTech Sport Tuning of California.

AutoTech front anti-roll bar kit comes complete with all fitting hardware for non-GTI models. You can use the factory brackets with Auto-Tech polyurethane bushes on a car already equipped with an anti-roll bar.

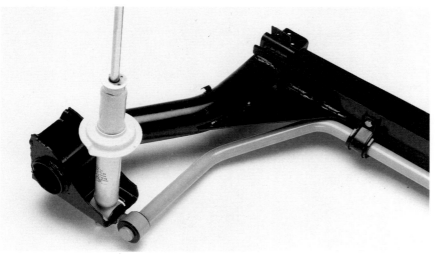

To prevent the rear anti-roll bar and the torsion beam axle fighting each other under deflection, AutoTech designed this 'popsicle' mount which uses the lower damper bolt as a locating point. It allows the bar to move in and out of the link to prevent binding, ensuring light loadings on the mounting points and linear geometry changes.

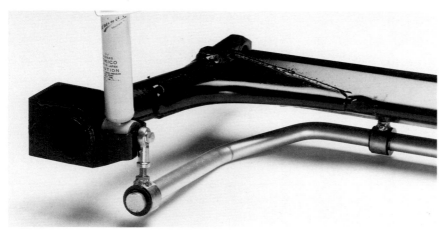

As the rear anti-roll bar on Mk2 cars is integral with the torsion beam, an additional bar has to be used to increase roll stiffness, rather than a replacement as on the Mk1. This is located under the torsion beam and connected to the damper bolts by drop links.

stiffness of the chassis without affecting suspension travel and thus ride comfort adversely. The AutoTech front anti-roll bar is a direct replacement for the factory original and comes with all the fitting hardware. The rear factory bar is part of the torsion beam assembly and thus upgrading it means adding an additional external bar. Such an external bar will have different pivot points from the torsion beam and, once the beam is deflected, this would cause the anti-roll bar to push or pull the end of the beam out of alignment. AutoTech's rear bars use a clever sliding end design to allow the beam to move properly and yet be usefully acted on by the anti-roll bar.

Stressbars: when a car is cornered hard, the forces produced by the act of the tyres gripping the road transmit high loadings back through the suspension to the monocoque bodyshell. Even though the mounting points are reinforced, the shell still deflects. A hatchback car with its large rear aperture is less rigid than a saloon, a convertible potentially even worse. When the shell deflects, it affects the suspension geometry, the accuracy of which is vital for good handling and grip. The Golf Mk1 shell is much less rigid than the Mk2 and the Cabriolet even weaker despite

substantial bracing to compensate for the loss of the roof. The Cabriolet also has a higher centre of gravity and so benefits even more from suspension bracing and uprating.

The weakest point of the Mk1 chassis is the lower front and the car benefits tremendously from a lower brace to stabilize the lower wishbone mountings. This has been done in more than one way by various manufacturers. The normal after-market European brace is a single bar which attaches to the front joints of both lower wishbones via the retaining bolts and then has two further bolts which attach it to the floorpan. Realising the weakness of the chassis, the factory developed a similar brace for the Scirocco 16V and this used a wholly tubular design with four mounting points which did the same job. Techtonics market a brace for the Mk1 cars which they admit is a direct copy of this.

The most comprehensive lower strut brace is the triangulated, fully adjustable one from AutoTech which is really a subframe. This connects the front and rear mounting points of the lower wishbones for maximum bracing and is then triangulated between front and rear bars. It is fully adjustable to take in the production tolerances of individual cars.

Although you can use a single bar to brace the front lower suspension arm mounts, a greater increase in stiffness is provided by a triangulated subframe like this one from AutoTech.

An upper shock-absorber tower brace for a Mk2. This looks after the structural integrity of the front end.

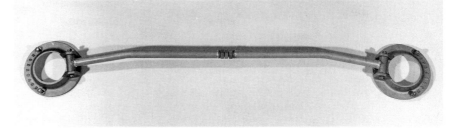

The Tarox slotted vented disc kit, a direct replacement for the standard front discs, improves pedal feel and reduces brake fade in hard driving. Unlike most competition-type brakes, it works perfectly from cold and does not make unpleasant noises.

A lower brace is more effective than an upper one on all Mk1-floorpan cars, ie Golf 1, Scirocco 1 and 2 and Jetta, but an upper shock tower brace is icing on the cake. The improvement in turn-in and cornering stability is instantly felt with the lower brace and steering becomes more positive. In the long term, the continuous loadings on the suspension strut towers weaken a car's structure. The upper stressbar helps to prevent this fatigue and staves off squeaks and rattles in higher-mileage cars. The Mk2 has a rigid front subframe from the factory and only needs a top stressbar.

As the rear torsion beam twists, so the loadings are transmitted to the bodyshell. A simple adjustable bar can be used to join the tops of the towers and this is easily removed when you need to use the car's full luggage carrying capacity. For more serious high-speed work, a multi-link triangulated set up is available from APS (Neuspeed) which has permanent fixtures in the bodywork via aircraft type Nutserts. The crossbrace, however, can still be removed.

Brakes

For owners of right-hand-drive Golf, Jetta and Scirocco cars with the Mk1 floorpan, brakes are rather a sore point. Because RHD was something of an afterthought, RHD cars retained their brake servo on the left-hand side of the bulkhead and the pedal action was transmitted via a bell crank linkage system with no less than eleven pivot

points! This was somewhat less effective than the system used by Ford with their Escort or by BMW in their contemporary cars, and left VW owners with a rather dead-feeling pedal and brakes that seemed inadequate for the car's performance. Although you could take up the slack in the linkage, it soon loosened again and you would end up adjusting it every three months or so.

Various solutions to the problem were tried. GTI Engineering would tighten up the linkage and fit Mintex M171 racing pads in the early days. This offered some improvement but the linkage would loosen with time and the racing pads, while they worked well when cold, unlike the Ferodo DS11s, would glaze-up easily in slow driving, made dreadful graunching noises when used hard and inevitably wore out the standard discs more quickly. At one point, GTI Engineering even tried grafting Ford Granada discs onto the Golf and these worked quite well but could only be used if you had 14in or larger diameter wheels fitted. It was also an expensive solution.

In 1985, the Italian brake maufacturer Tarox came on the scene with a replacement ventilated disc that was also slotted for better cooling and wear characteristics. With their own matching pads, this brake set worked very well and gave good stopping power, better pedal feel and superior fade characteristics. Tarox also make a set for the Mk2 Golf and, with the already satisfactory four-disc Mk2 set-up, this gives a

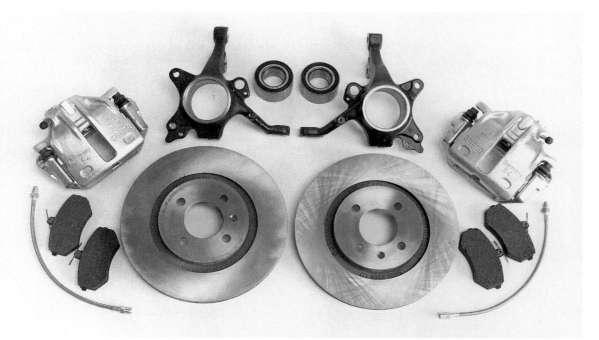

The ultimate in braking power, if you are prepared to go to 15in diameter wheels with 25 to 30mm offset, is provided by this APS/ Neuspeed 11in vented disc kit. These are essentially the G60 brakes, with all the parts you need to upgrade a Mk2 GTI or Jetta.

The APS/Neuspeed big-brake kit fitted to a Golf with Bilstein suspension. The kit includes a larger master cylinder and brake lines in Teflon and stainless steel.

GTI exceptional braking ability.

Grafting the rear discs from a Mk2 onto an earlier car is not a straightforward task. The hubs are different for a start. If you can find a crashed Scirocco 16V, it is easier just to swop rear axles and, of course, the brake proportioning valves have to be changed too.

While the initial idea was to get better pedal-feel and retardation by fitting larger discs to RHD cars, if LHD cars had satisfactory anchors with the same equipment, did it not make more sense to attack the problem at source? Autocavan certainly thought so and this British VW tuner sensibly brought out a stiffer, braced brake bar that fitted to the bulkhead and reduced the linkage pivot points to just two.

BR Motorsport's Brian Ricketts came up with a large servo conversion kit that raised brake line pressure considerably and gave a vastly better pedal feel. He also developed a bigger disc conversion. With both these modifications in place, he effectively put paid to the old joke, 'Why is a GTI like an Exocet? Because nothing will bloomin' well stop it!'

This did not mean that LHD markets were entirely happy with their brakes. When they uprated their engines, the American tuners sensibly looked for better stopping. AutoTech and APS offer big disc conversions for early and late GTI-based cars. Their latest kit uses the front discs from the G60 Corrado to stop the 170bhp turbocharged, supercharged or 2.0-litre cars they sell to clients. Buying a kit like this from these firms is very cost effective because not only do you get all the parts you need, and even Aeroquip braided hoses if you specify them, but, because of the quantities they buy from original equipment manufacturers, these tuners are able to offer the kits for about two-thirds the price you would pay if you assembled all the parts yourself from your local VW dealer.

Engine tuning

The basic VW water-cooled single-overhead-camshaft engine has proven very amenable to tuning for more power and torque. It is a simple and strong engine, coupled to a very robust gearbox that is able to take the output of forced aspiration engines, unlike some competitors' products which are more obviously built down to a price. The fact that the basic design started off as a 1.5-litre carburettor-equipped engine and has

now ended up being taken to over 2 litres (albeit based on an evolution block) speaks volumes for the rightness of the basic design. From a 1,471cc 70bhp engine, over 200bhp has been extracted in road-going, naturally aspirated form and nearly 300bhp with nitrous oxide injection. Road-going forced aspiration engines give anything from 160bhp to 250bhp, with massive torque.

If anything, the VW engine starts off with one basic disadvantage; it does not have a crossflow head design on its eight-valve version. A crossflow head, where the intake and exhaust tracts are on opposite sides, is logical for optimum gas flow, but the eight-valve engine lacks this refinement. For all that, it gives no ground to its obvious competitors, and in smoothness, power and torque delivery, it was the class standard for many years. The increased efficiency of the Oettinger and VW factory 16-valve crossflow heads reaped immediate rewards in power and torque and it is this newer version of the same basic engine that will take the GTI-based cars into the 1990s.

Brian Ricketts of BR Motorsport was the former Engineering Director of GTI Engineering, and the first British engineer to do serious modification work on the GTI back in 1977. According to Brian, the 1.6-litre engine was over-engineered for the task it had to perform. Not having done such a car before, VW erred on the side of strength. Brian remembers building a 182bhp car,

A good example of a car which has received the full benefit of the tuner's art is this Mk1 which John Boucoyannis built from a new shell. A marriage of the best of European and American tuning parts, this car sits on 7J x 15in ATS wheels with 195/50VR15 Pirelli P7 tyres.

Under the bonnet is a BR Motorsport 1,802cc engine giving 180bhp. This can be boosted to 240bhp or 290bhp with a two-stage nitrous oxide injection system. All fluid lines are metal braided. Note the Neuspeed strut brace.

Under the front end can be seen an Abt Tuning finned alloy sump and within is a Quaife torque-sensing limited-slip differential. The lower suspension arms are alloy ones from a Porsche 944 Turbo: these are the same shape and size as the Golf arms but the mounts have to be modified. The front sub-frame is the adjustable tri-angulated AutoTech item, and the anti-roll bar is from Neuspeed.

back in 1979, that revved to 8,500rpm. The internals had no special toughening or crank hardening. All that was done was a blueprint and balance. This car was a Group 2 European Saloon Car Championship runner. There are no particular major problems with the engine, says Brian, apart from the fact that, as they get older, some heads tend to crack between the valve seats. Sometimes blocks crack at the ends between the oil drain holes and head studs, but we are talking of massive mileages, between 80,000 and 100,000 miles. Of all the engines, the 110bhp 1.6 is potentially the most reliable because it is the simplest of the lot with the least moving parts.

The early 1.8-litre engines had head gasket problems but this was cured by changing the head

bolt torque-down sequence. Valve guides on these engines could also give way at around 30,000 miles or less. The material was subsequently changed, and longer guides used to prevent the valves 'walking about' on the seats. Usually though, problems with GTI engines are not failings of the engine but of ancillaries, especially those with electronic control systems. The 16-valve car is a favourite here as it can suffer from idle-stabilization circuit problems. Sometimes these are erratic and hard to trace. In 1984 cars, the wiring for the idle-stabilization circuit was too short and, with engine movement under acceleration and braking, it tended to chafe where it went through the bulkhead.

The 1.6-litre GTI engine is identified by the

With up to 290bhp on tap, you have to be able to stop effectively. The car has huge AP slotted, vented and drilled racing discs with four-pot calipers. The suspension stuts are Leda 22-point adjustable pattern.

The rear brakes are factory Scirocco 16V type – the rear axle was grafted in complete – and these have been drilled and grooved too. The brake pads are Tarox. The rear anti-roll bar with drop links is a Neuspeed item and the exhaust has a Supertrap racing silencer.

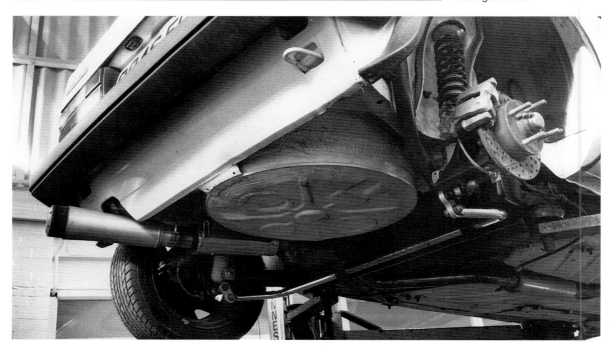

A serious weekend competition machine, John's Golf has an adjustable brake-bias control in the cockpit.

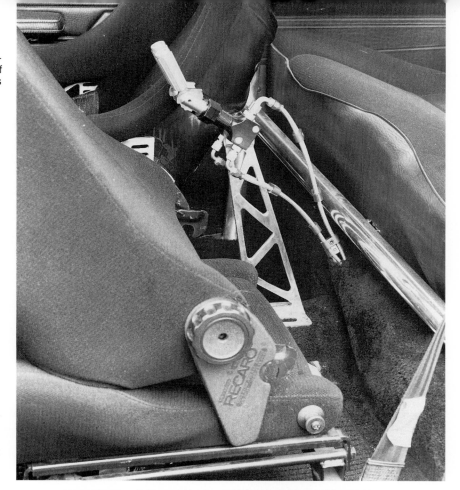

Open the rear hatch and you can see the Neuspeed rear shock-absorber tower brace, the nitrous oxide bottles and the cross-braces of the stout competition roll cage from Aleybars.

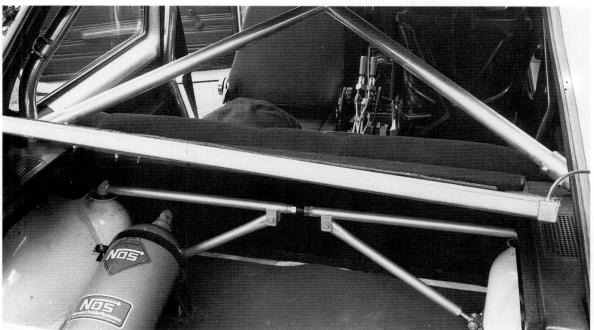

The driver is firmly located in a racing Recaro seat. The drilled competition pedal set is made in Japan but US-sourced through Flofit.

EG code stamped on the block. The Mk1 1.8-litre engine is a DX, the Mk2 an EV and the Digifant injection cars are denoted by the PB mark. The 16-valve is the KR series.

When you open up the 1.6 and 1.8-litre engines, the chief difference you will notice is in the combustion chamber design. The 1.6 has a flat head with the combustion chambers wholly in the piston tops. This design is akin to the racing VW engines and is preferred by tuners. The 1.8-litre engine's combustion chambers are shared by the head and the piston tops. The early Mk2 1.8-litre engines and then the 1984-onward DX engines in the Scirocco used air-shrouded injectors to clean up the idle mixture for smoother running, cleaner emissions and better fuel economy. These air-shrouded injectors gave better atomization and had idle air coming down the air rail when the throttle was closed. The air travelled through a bypass into the head which shut off as soon as the throttle was opened.

Another change around this time was the move from a direct oil-to-air oil cooler to a water-to-air one. The water-to-air oil cooler aids the initial heating of the engine oil with resultant shorter engine warm up. This also meant that the engine could come off its cold-start cycle faster with a resultant reduction in emissions and fuel consumption.

In late 1985, eight-valve cars went over to hydraulic tappets which were in fact the same as those used on the Mercedes-Benz 190E 2.3-16 and later the Cosworth Sierra. With the valve spring platform sunk further into the head, these engines had shorter valves. In service, they work very well with an extremely low failure rate.

On the induction side of things, the change from DX to EV 1.8-litre engines was marked by a re-arrangement of the air-flow meter box to the other side of the engine. A larger air-filter (same size as the Ford Capri 2.8 injection) was used and the compound throttle body was changed from a 38/45mm unit to the Audi-type 38/52mm unit. The longer inlet tract gave it better torque characteristics to pull the now larger car, rather than going for greater horsepower.

When the 16-valve engine first came out, there were complaints that cars did not meet their performance claims. Early cars had 44mm diameter intake runners and the factory enlarged these to 50mm which improved matters somewhat. US-spec cars with their emission-controlled engines

The Quaife torque-sensing limited-slip differential contains a series of helical gears which adjust automatically and progressively for loss of traction. It does not set up the kind of wheel-snatch that older LSDs can provoke in front-wheel-drive cars.

Of critical importance in any high-performance engine is the cylinder head. Despite not having a fashionable crossflow design, the eight-valve GTI engine gives nothing away to any of its competitors and is still near the top of the class in refinement.

and 123bhp come with this smaller diameter manifold, so a quick power boost can be achieved by using the 50mm Euro manifold. It is not cheap however, and on the Corrado, the 44mm manifold is used again.

On the exhaust side, the factory cast iron manifold on 1.6 and early 1.8-litre engines is not badly restrictive. Careful machining can produce good flow improvements and a swop to a four-branch extractor may not be as significant as with some other manufacturers' engines. One gaff the

factory made with the early 16V engines was the horrible conical exhaust downpipe that was internally split in the middle 60mm down. For the 1986 model year, they reverted to the twin downpipe. The conical downpipes also suffered badly from cracking.

The cylinder head of the Digifant-equipped car is unchanged apart from the holes for the injectors which are smaller. In South Africa, a 2-litre version of the 16-valve engine has gone into production to make up for the power loss

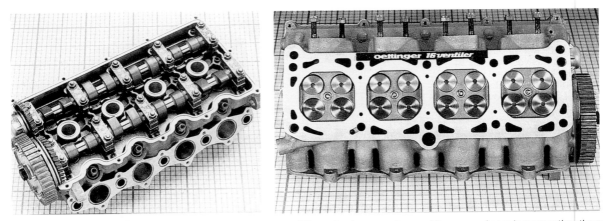

The Oettinger 16-valve cylinder head differs from the later VW version in several ways. The second cam is gear rather than chain-driven. But they share the crossflow layout and improved breathing which dramatically improve efficiency.

This Oettinger 16-valve conversion on a GTI Mk1 was done by GTI Engineering and shows how different the manifold architecture is from that of the later factory 16-valve unit.

experienced at the high altitude on the reef. This 2-litre block was first put in the heavier Passat in Europe, with a catalytic convertor. In this form, it produces 136bhp at 5,800rpm and 134lb/ft of torque at 4,400rpm. Because there are not the same strict emission laws in South Africa as in Europe, the factory there has been able to tune the 2-litre engine for over 150bhp: in any case they cannot use the catalyst equipped G60 engine as there is no lead-free fuel available. As far as Europe is concerned, for the time being, such an engine would be too close in power output to the

G60 cars, but this does not mean we might not see the 136bhp high-torque version of the 2-litre in the Golf GTI in the future.

In pure engineering terms, the 2-litre block is an improvement. It is a development of the KR 16V block with its front machined to fit the breather box. There is 5mm more clearance inside the block with the bore centres being spaced out slightly more. The intermediate gear shaft is smaller and the oil pump drive is bigger to give more crankshaft clearance. The oil feed system is superior, with oil jets from the main gallery squirting oil onto the undersides of the pistons. In previous modified 1.8 engines taken out to 2 litres, the bottoms of the pistons would foul the oil jets if you installed the system. Now, all 2-litre conversions use the Passat block as a starting point.

Internally, the chief difference between the 1.6 and 1.8-litre engines was in the combustion chambers. The 1.6 had a flat head with the chambers in the piston tops, while the 1.8 had chambers partly in the head and partly in the pistons.

Comparison of the early (top) and late intake manifolds for the factory 16-valve engine. The 50mm design gives significantly better gas flow than the earlier 44mm unit.

Engine modifications for increased power fall into four main categories: minor tweaks; bolt-on components; internal work; and, assuming you don't already own a G60, adding forced induction. Nowadays, emission-control legislation is increasingly complex and restrictive in many countries, though as yet less so in the UK than in many other places. While power tuning an engine, if well done, can keep it as 'clean' as the standard specification, this is not always achieved. If you live in a country or state where the limits are tight, it is important to check that any modifications you plan to make to your car are not going to bring you into conflict with the law.

Minor tweaks: whether you own a new or used GTI, it is amazing just how much improvement you can often gain simply by having the engine tuned to the optimum manufacturers' standard specification. The engines are very sensitive to correct fuel/air ratios, and it is almost impossible for a dealer without a rolling-road facility to set up an injected car with 100% accuracy. The static CO setting can be corrected at idle with an exhaust-gas analyser, but what the car does under load may be entirely different.

It is not uncommon for a car referred to a dealer with a complaint of lack of power to be found to have a perfect CO reading at idle. On a rolling road, however, it turns out to be running lean at the top end. This can be very bad for the engine, causing pinking or detonation; in extreme cases the mixture can be weak enough to cause a holed piston if the car were to be driven flat out for a short period. Production tolerances in the injection system, and perhaps too the effects of wear, mean that some cars remain correctly tuned while others cannot be set rich enough under full load. The difference can mean one car giving its full 112bhp while another produces perhaps only 95bhp.

Bolt-on components: basically, the car needs more fuel under load and one way to achieve this is to fit a modified warm-up regulator with a vacuum take-off in the intake plenum. Under full manifold depression, this squirts extra fuel into the system to restore power. The alternative is a rising-rate fuel pressure regulator which increases fuel pressure upon demand. Both these methods work well because they supply extra fuel only under load, whereas if you simply raise the fuel pressure or modify the air metering flap, you alter the whole fuel-delivery curve and make the engine run over-rich at low speeds.

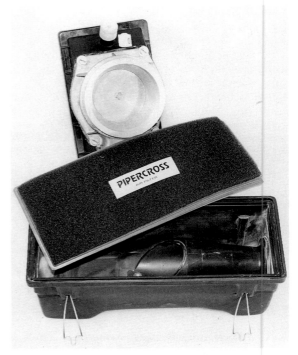

A good-quality air filter will allow the engine to breathe better while making sure no abrasive particles reach the working surfaces.

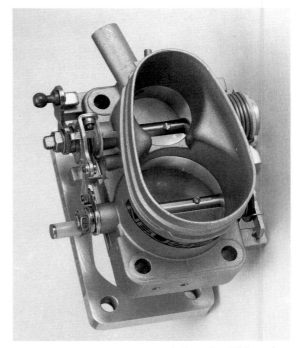

The larger 38/52mm throttle body from the Mk2 car is a worthwhile retrofit for any Mk1 1.6 or 1.8 GTI engine.

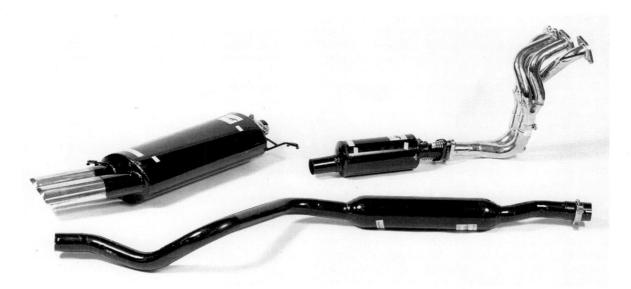

A good aftermarket exhaust system has a four-into-two-into-one manifold and a set of efficient silencers to increase power without making the car noisier. You can gain at least 10bhp and sharper throttle response. This system for a Scirocco 16V is by the Italian maker, Supersprint.

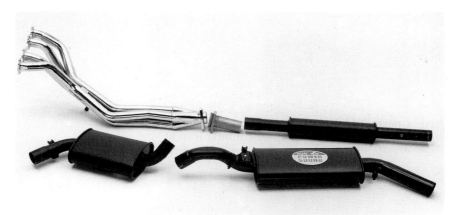

This replacement exhaust system from Gillet is for a Golf Mk2.

Getting more air in will give a useful power increase. For that reason, the large throttle body is a good upgrade for Mk1 cars. Also, a free-flow air filter from a reputable manufacturer like K&N or Pipercross will help the engine breathe better while keeping damaging dirt particles out. You can even drill holes in the bottom of the air box to increase flow, but if you do, make sure you change the filter more frequently. You will also have to suffer more induction noise.

More air needs more fuel if you are to keep the mixture correct. If your system is borderline, as explained already, it will now definitely need modification. Assuming the correct mixture balance, a good air filter is worth an extra one or two bhp.

Restricted air flow into the engine is one limiting factor on its performance; exhaust back-pressure on the way out is another. A good extractor manifold helps gases get away quickly and is worth a few bhp. It works best if used with a complete free-flow system like those made by Super Sprint, Jetex, Leistritz, Gillet, Ansa Sebring or Hor Technologie. A good-quality system may cost more to start with but if it gives more power and lasts longer it is an investment. The basic requirement for a good manifold is that the four pipes should merge gently; the real subtlety comes in achieving this without abrupt changes in cross-sectional area. This allows the gases an easy path and creates less adverse turbulence.

Internal work: porting and polishing cylinder heads and manifolds is looked upon as a black art by some. It is really a common-sense operation, but one in which the skill of the operator is still at a premium so that certain gifted technicians do better than others. Even after optimum port and chamber design using a Superflow flow bench, I have seen the work of two different machinists produce different power outputs from visually identical heads!

It is more important to port-match manifolds to the head than to polish them. The sparkling smooth inlet manifolds you see at shows are not in practice the best thing for power production, because polished tracts tend to 'wet out' with fuel droplets, especially where the atomization path is fairly long. This happens more with carburettors than fuel injection. So it is best to have a slightly matt surface. Port matching is important so that mixture flow and then exhaust gas flow is as smooth and unimpeded as possible. Smooth and shaped combustion chambers that induce enough turbulence to achieve more efficient mixture burn are a great help, while reprofiling of the valves and valve seats to get mixture velocity up and spent gases out should be aimed for.

As with most engines, useful power is to be found in the heads. The 16-valve head can be cleaned up and flowed to give an improvement in inlet and exhaust flow rates of as much as 24% and 44% respectively. With reshaped valves, this work is worth nearly 20bhp. There is an engineering formula that states the ideal relationship between inlet and exhaust valve sizes, and by taking the inlet valves from 32 to 34mm and the exhaust valves from 28 to 28.5mm significant increases in power and low-speed torque are achieved. Note how small in real terms the enlargements are. While valves that are too small strangle the flow in the head, you have to be very careful with valve sizes because you can reach a situation where over-large valves give you a worse result through reduction in gas flow velocity.

As far as the use of lead-free petrol is concerned, all GTI-type engines can use lead-free as they have hardened valve seats. What has kept VW from allowing owners to use lead-free on 16V cars in the UK up to now was the non-availability of high-octane (97 RON) lead-free. It

Comparison of European and US-specification GTI pistons: the high compression (10:1) piston is on the left.

Cast and forged pistons for the 16-valve engine: the forged piston is on the right.

was a matter of octane rather than lead content. The fuel catalyst Carbonflo, however, has been tested and proven to allow the use of normal 95 octane lead-free in 16-valve GTI engines with no loss of power or chance of damage. There is thus nothing to stop GTI drivers from being environmentally conscious.

It is quite common for enthusiasts to have gas flowing, porting and polishing done and then a free-flow exhaust fitted. The step beyond this, though, takes the owner into a realm where serious money has to be spent. The old adage 'there is no substitute for cubic inches' still holds true today, and when it comes to making effortless power, there is no other recourse but to enlarge engine capacity for torque – unless you are willing to resort to supercharging or turbocharging.

Engine response is directly linked to compression ratio which is why race cars run compression ratios far beyond the 10:1 that is the normal

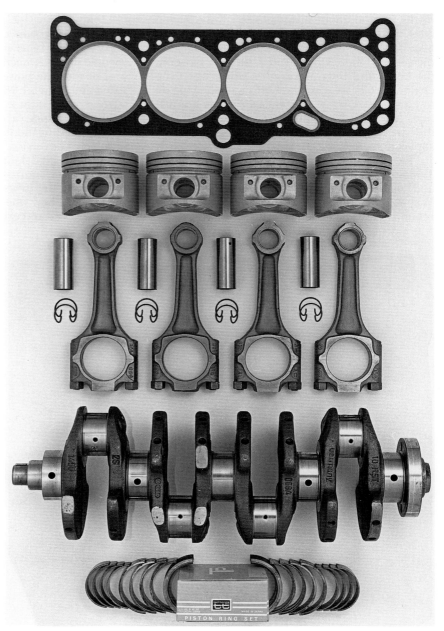

All the parts needed to turn a 1,781cc engine into a torquey and free-revving 1,870cc unit. This is the Techtonics conversion: Darrell Vittone of Techtonics is the USA's guru of GTI tuning.

maximum for road cars given the quality of today's pump petrol. Note, though, that really wild camshaft profiles with a lot of overlap reduce the effective compression ratio whatever the simple volumetric figure may be, so that the compression figures you see for out-and-out racing engines are not always directly comparable with road-car power units. US specification cars run 8.5:1 compression ratios compared to 10:1 on Euro GTIs. A good upgrade with an engine capacity increase is thus high-compression pistons. There are a lot of myths around about pistons. Yes, all the racing boys used forged pistons, but they are not necessarily the best thing for road use. Because they expand more when heated, they are looser in the bores and thus make more noise when the engine is cold, wearing the bores and allowing oil to blow past. For road use, cast pistons are just fine. All GTIs have forged steel crankshafts, so they are as strong as they need to be for any road application.

One of the favourite early conversions takes the 1,588cc engine to 1,847cc by boring it to 82.5mm and using a long-stroke 86.4mm crankshaft. When you consider that a complete engine rebuild involves a certain amount of labour, doing such a conversion on a high-mileage engine is a worthwhile alternative to straightforward reconditioning. The capacity increase is worth 15bhp and, combined with head work, change of camshaft and valve work, BR Motorsport claim 140bhp at the flywheel for such an engine.

For cars that start off with the 1,781cc block, an 1,870cc conversion using the standard stroke of 86.4mm and 83.0mm oversize pistons gives a more oversquare and freer-revving engine. With modified head, cam and balancing, this gives 142bhp and a lot more low-speed torque. A similar conversion on a 16-valve unit is worth 170bhp and is as powerful an engine as most people will ever need.

For ultimate power, the 2-litre Passat block is used and, with a 1,984cc capacity from a bore and stroke of 82.5mm x 92.8mm, 190bhp is possible with head work, a camshaft change and other minor modifications. The largest commercially available conversion for a 1.8-litre GTI engine is the AutoTech 2.1-litre kit which has an 84.0mm bore and 92.8mm stroke for 2,057cc. In eight-valve form, this gives 150bhp and with a 16-valve head, 170bhp, when used with an AutoTech cylinder head and exhaust. The kit uses the 2-litre

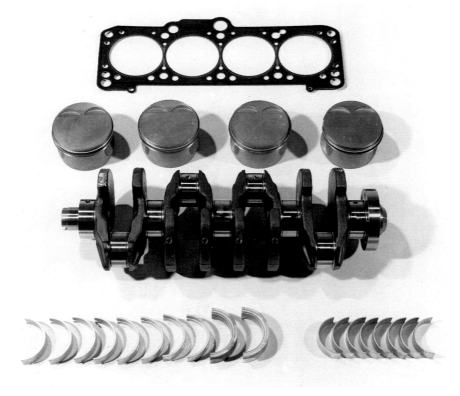

The largest capacity engine you can make from a 1.8-litre GTI unit is 2,057cc. This AutoTech kit provides the necessary parts.

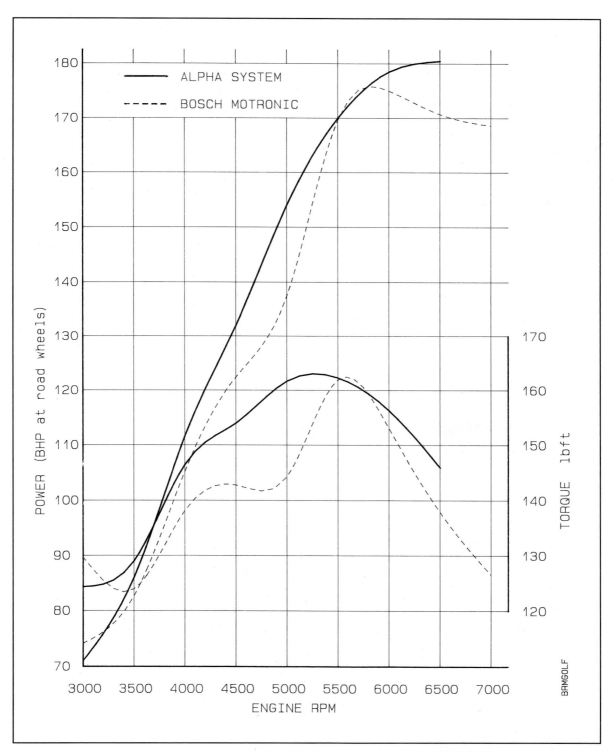

This graph compares the power and torque characteristics of a BR Motorsport BRM180 2-litre engine fitted with Bosch K-Jetronic injection against the same engine with the Weber Alpha electronic engine management system. The figures speak for themselves.

Passat crankshaft, AutoTech/Mahle oversized cast pistons, new bearings and a special head gasket. For the 16-valve engine you also get a set of reduced-height oil squirters, necessary because of the size of the crankshaft. (This would not be necessary if you started with a 2-litre Passat block, but the gains from an extra 70cc are not worth the cost of a new block.) ABT Tuning in Germany do a similar engine for which they claim 180bhp. Master of the big-engine conversions in the USA is the Riverside-based company Techtonics, run by long-time VW tuner and GTI guru Darrell Vittone.

So far, the most powerful naturally aspirated road-going GTI around was done by BR Motorsport and Weber distributor Auto Technique of Luton for Glyn Jones. The Weber Alpha engine management system was added to a BR Motorsport 2-litre engine and this has endowed the car with 205bhp at 6,500rpm at the flywheel, 181bhp at the front wheels, and a whopping 163lb/ft of torque at 5,250rpm. The important thing is how well the Weber system has filled out the troughs in the power and torque curves compared to the already well tuned BRM 180 car. With ever-tightening emission laws, this kind of fully programmable engine management looks like becoming *the* tuners' accessory of the near future.

Camshafts: most of the larger tuners are now producing tuned cars with catalytic convertors, giving increased power without affecting emission levels. Valve timing is a critical factor in the power vs emissions balance. Camshafts with too much overlap let through a lot of unburnt fuel and are therefore 'dirty'. The famous German camshaft manufacturer Schrick does a range of camshafts for catalyst-equipped cars.

A larger-capacity engine can take a cam with a longer duration. Thus while a 260-degree duration cam may be very wild for a 1.6-litre car, it is mild when used on a 2-litre version of the same engine. Experience has shown that, for normal road driving, that 260-degree cam in a 2-litre car has such a nice civilized feel, near-stock idle – and yet so much pulling power. Anything wilder produces a car with a frustrating lack of bottom-end torque.

Many people rely too much on 0-60mph and top speed figures as a guide to a car's performance. A slightly slower car in these terms which has more torque and is faster from, say, 30-50mph and 50-70mph will be quicker and less tiring to drive in give-and-take traffic and fast country-road conditions. Remember, bhp gives you top speed but torque gives you acceleration. Your exit speed from a corner defines your speed down the straight. Therefore, a car with good handling and grip and plenty of torque will always score over the screamer whose power is all at the top end. A torquey car that does not have to work so hard will also reward you at the petrol pump.

Forced induction: the robust Golf engine responds well to turbocharging, and with a good installation, as done by Callaway in the US and Turbo Technics in Britain, you will find a turbo GTI just like the standard car in terms of drivability, only much more powerful. The fact that the intake and exhaust are on the same side on

This is the Golf GTI of Glyn Jones, powered by a BRM180 engine with the Weber Alpha system, a combination which produces 205bhp.

Under the bonnet of the Glyn Jones GTI. The torque and smoothness of this engine are most impressive.

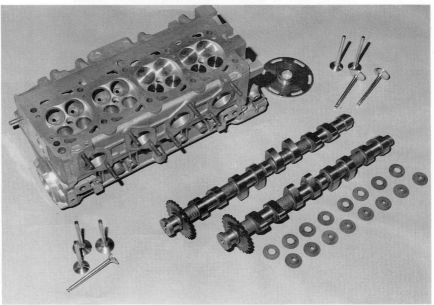

This is the cylinder head of the BRM180 2-litre conversion showing the modified ports, combustion chambers and valves, and the Schrick 260-degree cams.

the eight-valve engine means that the heat reflective shielding has to be carefully done to prevent fuel vaporization taking place. Apart from that, careful routing of intercooler pipes and casting of a high-quality exhaust manifold to take the turbo are the main design problems a turbo installer will encounter. The excellent chassis of the GTI-type cars require less uprating to take the power of a turbo than some other hot hatchbacks and, on the whole, power increases to between 150bhp and 190bhp are reasonable for road use.

If you have four-wheel drive, you can afford to turn the wick up higher, as Abt Tuning did with their turbocharged 220bhp 16-valve engined syncro. This is the sort of power that would not go very well in a car with just front-wheel drive. Really pushing the limits of a front-driven Corrado chassis is the Oettinger five-valve-per-cylinder engine. Shown at the 1989 Frankfurt IAA Show, the new head has three inlet and two exhaust valves on a 1,760cc (81.0mm x 86.4mm) engine block. Turbocharged, this engine gives 250bhp at 6,200rpm and torque is a phenomenal 214lb/ft at 2,500rpm. It is likely that wheelspin limits the Corrado's 0-60mph time to 6.1

seconds. Top speed is 162mph! With the normal four-valve head on his engine, Treser claims 240bhp and a 158mph top speed for his Corrado. 0-60mph is similar to the Oettinger car.

Supercharging, popular for aviation piston-engines in the last war and for cars in the 1920s and 1930s, is making a comeback. VW is the first major manufacturer to produce a supercharged car in the second half of the 20th century, but even before the debut of their G60 models, several aftermarket tuners had had a go. Nothelle tried a 150bhp car back in 1984/5, as did Brian Ricketts

This turbo installation for a 1.8-litre Mk1 was developed in South Africa and produced a staggering 197bhp. Note the fabricated strut brace between the top damper mounts.

Another South African conversion was this GTI, turbocharged by its owner. The power output was boosted to 170bhp.

This is the 220bhp turbo-charged 16-valve engine of the Abt Tuning Golf syncro. Forced induction makes the most of the gas flow advantages conferred by the multi-valve head.

The Oettinger *five*-valves-per-cylinder head was shown at the 1989 Frankfurt Show. Audi are reported to be almost at production stage with a five-valve head, too, so this configuration could well be the next trend.

German tuners Nothelle experimented with supercharging back in 1985 and were getting over 150bhp from this Golf.

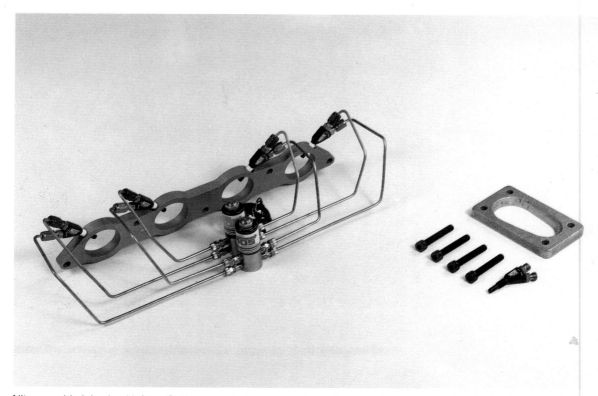

Nitrous oxide injection kit for a Golf as sold by AutoTech. Dramatic power increases can be obtained for short bursts of acceleration.

when he was with GTI Engineering. In Britain also, Steiner Engineering built a 160bhp supercharged car using American parts from Auto-Tech, with limited success. Supercharging scores for its instant response and superb low-end lugging power. The cars are not dramatically quick off the line, but it is in mid-range acceleration, as when overtaking, that you reap the benefits. As with turbocharging, you need to lower the compression ratio and control the whole fuelling and ignition set-up, electronically if possible, for optimum performance and knock resistance. It would be interesting indeed if the Weber Alpha system could be applied to a supercharged version of the GTI engine.

Nitrous Oxide, chemical symbol NO_2, is 32% oxygen by weight and is compressed and stored in a gas bottle at -178 degrees C. When it is injected into an engine, it vaporizes and takes the heat from the incoming atmospheric air. The extra oxygen present combines with extra fuel in the combustion chambers and gives a great increase in power. A 'fogger nozzle', which mixes the NO_2 and fuel, is placed next to the throttle body on the inlet plenum at a calculated distance to provide optimum atomization. In stage one on a 180bhp 1,802cc Golf, the power increase is around 40bhp.

In stage two, four fogger nozzles are used, one next to each inlet tract. It is vital to ensure that each cylinder gets the same amount. On a test vehicle, stage two was worth an extra 70bhp. When this is in use, the ignition timing has to be retarded. NO_2 can only be used for acceleration runs both because of the limited size of the gas bottle and because it should only be used on full throttle if you are not to damage the engine. It is a cheap way to get dramatic power increases, but you must ensure the system is installed properly and that the engine is healthy enough to take the strain of the dramatic increase in output.

Carburettors: last but not least, and perhaps an unlikely end to the engine tuning section of a book on a fuel-injected car, it is worth noting how effective carburettors are on a GTI. When VW first started experimenting with the Sport Golf, they tried the 100bhp carburettor engine from the Audi 80GT and pronounced it not powerful

Installing two twin-choke Weber carburettors may sound like a good old tuner's recipe from days gone by, but it has been proved effective on both eight and 16-valve GTI engines. This GMP Scirocco with Zender styling made nearly 150bhp this way, with suitable cam and exhaust mods. One choke per cylinder is great for power and torque but fuel economy and low emissions go out of the window.

Opposite and above, this Corrado developed by Turbo Technics has its 16V engine fed through an intercooler by a Garrett T25 turbocharger. A two-stage boost control allows the driver to select 0.4bar and 140bhp or 0.65bar and 188bhp. Power delivery is strong and seamless with 160lb/ft of torque available at just 3,500rpm. A digital control unit adjusts fuel mixture, boost pressure and ignition timing for optimum settings at all times. The wheels are from Zender and suspension modifications were done by Steiner Engineering.

enough. From there on, the K-Jetronic injection system was adopted. But for ultimate power, there is no substitute for a single choke per cylinder, which is why the Weber Alpha injection system using bespoke single throttle bodies mounted on Weber DCOE carburettor manifolds is so effective. If you are not concerned with drivability, consumption or emissions, then sticking a pair of DCOE Weber carbs on a 2-litre 16-valve GTI engine is an interesting way to find 140-150bhp with the noise to match. If the head, cams and exhaust are done too, this motor should be good for 180-190bhp with plenty of torque in the narrow band when it is on cam.

The ultimate innocent-looking Q-car was produced for a customer by London-based Steiner Engineering, who built a 16-valve carburettor-fed engine into a five-door Golf 1.3 GL bodyshell. Standard on the outside apart from wider wheels and tyres, this 150bhp monster has the full AutoTech/Hor/Tokico suspension, strut brace and anti-roll bar set-up installed as well as heavy duty brakes. BMW 325is and Porsche 944s do not know what hit them!

9

Lasting impressions

As modern cars have become more and more competent and refined, they have tended also to become more and more devoid of character. While this may not bother most of the people who buy them – salesmen, executives, housewives, to whom a car is primarily a way of getting from A to B – it is a vital loss to anyone who considers himself or herself an enthusiastic driver. How refreshing, then, to find a thoroughly modern and well engineered car which feels as though it is meant to be enjoyed, not just used. In this respect, the high-performance VWs excel. Their engines and drivetrains positively encourage hard driving and, at the end of the day, they will come back for more when rivals are wilting under the strain. The build quality and durability of VW products is such that they can withstand hard driving – short of actual abuse – for very high mileages. Members of the press are not kind to cars when it comes to taking performance figures and assessing handling and grip at test tracks and it is notable that a VW that has covered the customary 12-15,000 miles before it is removed from the press fleet is still as taut and rattle-free as the day it left the factory. We have noticed various vehicles from rival manufacturers feeling distinctly loose and worn after 15,000 miles of such treatment.

Golf GTI
The first time I drove a Golf GTI in the late 1970s, I knew I had found the car I was looking for. Up to that point, I had had various Italian sporting coupes that were fun to drive but had horrendous build quality, poor reliability and rust problems. The smoothness, tractability and will-ingness to rev of the GTI's 1.6-litre engine were almost unbelievable after the hiccups of car-burettored Italian machinery, and the doors closed with a bank-vault quality that promised a lasting relationship.

What was immediately apparent was that this little nugget of a car was exactly as big as it had to be and had the handling and grip to match its performance. It was the perfect size to negotiate London traffic and nip into parking spaces that were denied to small BMWs and, at the same time, its hatchback with folding rear seats made it an extremely useful car for carrying 'tools of the trade' or simply for an extended tour of the Continent. No wonder then, that the GTI, especially in black, soon became the pet of the Chelsea and Kensington set in London and ultimately the supreme 'yuppie' car across the globe. That type-casting was most unfortunate though, for the GTI, tame enough as it was to perform mundane urban duties, really came into its own on the open road where its sharp handling, small size and superb power-to-weight ratio made it an agile cross-country runner. It was equally at home on motorways and could run nearly flat-out for hours on end thanks to a strong engine and an oil cooler. It was unfortunate that the body structure and drivetrain conspired to create a boom in the rear of the cabin which was irritating to rear seat passengers. This happened at about 70mph, the British speed-limit on motorways, and meant that more serene progress was made above or below this speed.

The engine of the GTI 1600 felt almost unburstable. It would start first turn of the key even if the car had been lying idle for weeks and, once warmed through, would pull to the red-line like a turbine, accompanied by a lovely rorty exhaust note. The gearchange quality was also excellent. The short stubby lever in the later five-speed cars was like a big flick-switch. With comparatively short movements across and up and down the box, it was a joy to blast this car along twisty A and B roads. The gear speeds were perfectly chosen: the five close ratios took up perfectly one after the other, producing one long blast of sustained acceleration if you did a standing-start to top speed run. Miss a gear, say if you went from third to fifth in normal driving to save on fuel, and you knew that the engine had dropped off the cam. In the more powerful 1,800cc version, you could do this with impunity as the extra torque covered the 'hole' in the gearbox that resulted from skipping a gear.

The GTI had two obvious dynamic failings, one minor and the other only manifest in right-hand-drive cars. The minor flaw in its dynamic makeup was that the rack-and-pinion steering was slightly vague about the straight ahead. Once through this 'loose' area though, it was nicely weighted and communicative. Right-hand-drive GTIs had to have a cross-linkage to couple the brake pedal to the servo on the left-hand side of the bulkhead. This had rather too many pivot points, and the whole arrangement introduced so much flexing and lost motion that the pedal feel on RHD cars gave great concern to fast drivers. Many aftermarket tuners attempted various combinations of discs and pads, but it was not until the problem was tackled at source, by improving the linkage and then fitting a bigger servo and discs, that a solution was found.

All cars based on the Mk1 floorpan also tend to hit their bumpstops on hard bumps taken at speed. This seems to be a characteristic of the wheel travel and suspension design on the Mk1 and is not cured even by fitting the progressively sprung Bilstein, Koni or Sachs spring and damper sport suspension.

If the opposition was getting as fast or faster in terms of raw power, as 1982 drew to a close, VW

A Mk1 car showing the rear wheel lift characteristic of all GTIs under hard cornering. It looks more dramatic than it feels, and remains safe and controllable.

The longer-wheelbase Mk2 is more stable in hard cornering especially in the wet or on loose surfaces.

replied with the 1,781cc engine, offering just 2bhp more but with more torque in the low and mid engine-speed ranges. The bigger engine was not quite as sweet as the 1600, but it delivered the goods in a more relaxed manner and made for an easier car to drive swiftly. That extra torque was very telling when exiting corners. I remember testing a Toyota MR2 at Castle Combe circuit, where my times were just 1.5sec a lap slower than Chris Hodgetts, the Toyota saloon car racing champion in a Corolla GTi: the little Toyota was as fast as the GTI to 60mph and had a higher top speed but, coming out of the bends, a colleague in a Mk1 1800 GTI was pulling away quite noticeably, showing just how much torque counts in fast driving.

Golf GTI Mk2

The first Mk2 GTI I drove was a left-hand-drive car that had been personally imported to the UK. Coming out of a Mk1, you were instantly struck by the more solid and substantial feel of the newer car. It was much quieter and more comfortable on the road, showing how standards changed during the nine-year lifespan of the first Golf. Although the early Mk2 GTIs had a similar engine to the late Mk1 cars, small revisions to improve low-speed torque even further had left it a slightly lower-revving unit. Extra size and weight also made the car feel less nimble.

On the race track, though, the new car showed its edge. With a longer wheelbase, it was less prone to oversteer on throttle lift-off even though it would still lift its inside rear wheel off the ground in very hard cornering. The car felt more stable and was very forgiving even if its driver was not quite up to scratch. I remember one incident at a GTI Drivers' Club meet at Goodwood where one ham-fisted pilot got it totally wrong and went into a corner too fast (for him) and on the wrong line. Following behind, I saw him dangle a rear wheel in the air, lock up the other rear wheel in a puff of tyre smoke as he attempted to lose speed, and more or less manage to collect himself as the car barely deviated from its line. In many other cars, the driver would have left the corner backwards, but the GTI had enough in reserve to save its hapless driver from that ignominy.

Despite sporting spring and damper settings, the GTI Mk1 had a comfortable ride and the occasional bottoming out at the front was more heard than felt. The ride quality of the Mk2 was even better. The longer wheelbase made its contribution to stability and ride, and longer wheel travel in the suspension, with re-rated springs and dampers, resulted in a chassis that took all road surfaces in its stride. The most important thing for British owners, though, was that the RHD version had been designed-in right from the start. This meant that RHD cars had a different bulkhead with the brake servo moved accordingly, as well as a proper RHD wiper mounting too. With ventilated discs in front, and solid discs at the rear in place of the drums on the Mk1, the new GTI dramatically extended the braking confidence window for its drivers.

Golf GTI 16V

'The eight-valve GTI has more low down pulling power than the 16-valve.' Members of the press have said it and owners of eight and 16-valve GTIs have said it, but it is not actually true. The 16-valve car does have a slight cammy feel to it and seems to go harder once the 4,500rpm mark has been exceeded. This extra dose of power makes the car feel rather lethargic below that figure and gives the illusion that it is not as tractable as the eight-valve car which has a more seamless power delivery. In fact, if you compare the torque characteristics of the two engines, the 16-valve car never drops below 118lb/ft from 2,800 to 6,100rpm, while the eight-valver peaks at 111lb/ft at 3,100rpm.

But the characteristics of the two engines are completely different. The latest Digifant-injected eight-valve is even less of a revver than the early Mk2s on K-Jetronic. The car has much less snap than the Mk1 and in my personal opinion has become a better Golf but a less good GTI. The 16-valve, on the other hand, embraces the original formula of the Mk1 with a crisp power delivery, sporting response and the ability to rev cleanly to well over 6,000rpm.

The latest changes have in a sense widened the gap between the two cars in driver appeal. The 16-valve has stiffer suspension with better control which will appeal to the hard-charging enthusiast who likes to use the gears and high revs more. The eight-valver on the other hand is now a softer, more civilized car for the quieter driver who demands maximum tractability for town driving but wants a car that will perform well on the open road as well.

Golf G60

It may surprise many people to learn that the G60 GTI is actually slower than the 16V to 60mph although it has a higher top speed. Unlike the aftermarket turbocharged cars, the factory supercharged GTI does not greet your depressed right foot with an intoxicating rush of power; it is a far more progressive beast than that. For those who have revelled in the characteristics of a powerful turbocharged car, the rather laid-back G60 may well come as a disappointment. It is smooth and progressive and totally unobtrusive, although if you wind down the window you can share the odd-sounding whine with onlookers, for the G60-powered VWs sound like no other cars. Where the supercharger scores is in intermediate-gear acceleration and tractability.

With its lowered suspension and big wheels and tyres, the G60 has a higher level of grip on a smooth road than the 16-valve, and the latest power-steering set-up is a far cry from the over-light arrangement offered on the very early 16V

The ultimate production GTI in action. The lower stance and distinctive whine from the G-lader make the G60 instantly recognizable.

The G60 Limited Golf will only ever be experienced by a small group of GTI enthusiasts, but this discreet special with 210bhp and 4WD is the hottest hatchback made by any major manufacturer.

cars. The smooth surge of power from the G60 engine is very satisfying as you blast from corner to corner on a twisty road, and there is the feel, as with all GTIs, that the basic chassis is capable of handling even more power.

An interesting technical innovation VW launched with the Golf G60 was their Electronic Differential Lock (EDL) which uses the ABS sensors to detect variations in wheel speed. Unlike the BMW and Mercedes-Benz ASD systems which reduce engine power to compensate for lack of traction, the VW system works by slowing the wheels down. If you should encounter a puddle of water or loose gravel mid-bend, you will not get the dramatic loss of composure you might in a standard car. The system only works if there is a difference in speed between the driven wheels. So it is still possible to spin the wheels if both are on a surface of equal frictional coefficient. If you were to launch the car on a loose surface, you would thus spin the wheels, but the moment one wheel reached a grippy surface, the antics would be called to a halt.

The chassis of the GTI G60 is firm, make no mistake. This is not a soft-riding motorcar, and yet it never really jars your sensibilities. On a rough surface, you are left in no doubt that the car is firm, and the power steering provides plenty of feedback of information. The car's handling and grip are simply phenomenal. Helped by the EDL, it puts every one of the 160bhp down convincingly. If anything, grip with EDL has changed the handling of the standard car from understeer and lift-off tuck-in to understeer and then neutral. Those used to deliberately using the lift-off tuck-in of the normal GTI as a driving technique will get a fright the first time they try to induce that effect on an EDL-equipped G60. The only way to bring the tail round is to take a stab at the brakes to alter the weight transfer more dramatically.

A practical sporting car for open-air enthusiasts, the Golf Cabriolet combines the comforts of a saloon with the fun of a traditional open sports car.

Motorsport Golf Limited

If the Golf G60 feels as though its chassis could handle more power, the Limited provides that power in the form of 210bhp from a supercharged 16V engine. Wisely, VW elected to pair it with their syncro 4WD system. While the standard G60 unit merely enhances the tractability of the eight-valve engine, the 16-valve version releases the full potential of the supercharger system. Acceleration is vivid, with 60mph coming up in 7.0 seconds. But what is impressive is that the power never seems to tail off until you hit the rev limiter just past 7,000rpm. Get to 100mph ...

smooth onward urge. 186lb/ft of torque at 5,000rpm is 3-litre pulling power and, with the drive going to all four wheels, once the fronts begin to slip under the strain of the torque, the handling balance of this car is beyond the capabilities of a normal front-wheel-drive GTI. Power-on in a tight corner and the Limited adopts a more neutral stance and full throttle can be applied early once the car is settled. In wet corners, power sliding out on opposite lock is possible, another fun element denied to the FWD Golf enthusiast. For all that, the Limited is a refined and mature vehicle that cossets its

The Golf GTI is the cult car that has stolen most of the limelight, but the Jetta GTI and GTI 16V are superb drivers' cars in their own right and every bit the equal of the Golf on the road or race track.

120mph ... and it is still pulling hard. Very low down, the engine still does not have the razor-edge response of a good naturally aspirated unit. Frustratingly – because it is so good past 2,500rpm – it does take a fraction of a second to 'come to the boil' and really get going. This is probably a function of the lower compression ratio (compared to a stock 16V) and/or insufficient gas speed at low rpm, a problem with many multi-valve engines.

Once it starts to build up, though, it is intoxicating and you find yourself using the gears for the sheer exhilaration of feeling the strong and

occupants in its leather upholstery and pampers them with luxuries like electric windows, central locking and a sunroof.

Only 70 Motorsport Golf Limited cars were made, lovingly constructed by VW Motorsport personnel during 1990, but this wolf in sheep's clothing, looking just like any metallic black five-door Golf with a set of BBS wheels, is the ultimate hot-hatchback of its day just as surely as the original Golf GTI was. Advances in technology and in market conditions have created in this car a level of sophistication as telling today as that of the first GTI in 1975. Ironically, this Q-car shares one flaw with that original GTI: in its attempt to remain discreet in appearance, with just two headlamps, its night-driving capabilities are severely hampered.

Golf GTI Cabriolet

Just as the Golf GTI spawned many imitators such as the Escort XR3i and the Peugeot 205 GTi, so the success of the Golf Cabriolet pushed rival manufacturers to make open versions of their hot hatches. While the Mk2 Golf has pursued refinement in its chassis and overall deportment, the Carbriolet retains the more raunchy and vibrant feel of the original GTI. Because of this, it remains a better open-air fun car than its direct rivals. The engine of the Cabriolet is smooth, sweet and torquey and, when you have the hood down, the powerful rasp of the exhaust note under hard acceleration adds to the sensation of open-air motoring.

With more weight in the rear, the Cabriolet has a different handling balance from the GTI. Its tuck-in is more pronounced if you lift off the throttle at high cornering speeds and the way to avoid an oversteering situation is to flick the steering wheel straight as you lift off. For an open car converted from a saloon, the VW Cabriolet has good structural rigidity. Scuttle shake is detectable but it is not worrying. Acceleration and top speed are down on the GTI because of the extra weight and the blunter shape, but open-air motoring is not about flat-out driving: it is about enjoying the sights and sounds around you in a car that is tactile, responsive and civilized. The Golf Cabriolet has these attributes in full measure.

Jetta

The extra weight at the rear and thus the differently placed centre of gravity of the Jetta in both Mk1 and Mk2 forms creates a car with slightly different handling characteristics from the Golf. If you lift off on the limit in a Jetta, the oversteer tendency is greater, especially if the boot is loaded. Driving an empty Jetta GTi 16V back-to-back with a Golf GTI 16V at Donington circuit one morning, it quickly became apparent that the different balance of the Jetta in fact helped to cut understeer and made the car turn-in better. From a driver's point of view, this can be quite desirable. In terms of grip, the two cars are pretty evenly matched but I suspect that in steady-state cornering on a skidpan, the Golf would ultimately produce a higher lateral g figure as it would not move into oversteer so quickly.

Driving both cars around Oulton Park, a hilly circuit with several fast dips and crests, I was impressed with how well the Golf and Jetta handled with four people on board. Both cars could comfortably be driven on the limit in this load configuration with extremely safe and stable track manners. Many good road cars lose their composure rapidly when subjected to the rigours of on-the-limit driving around a racing circuit. The Golf and Jetta and of course their Scirocco and Corrado stablemates are rare cars that offer equally exemplary behaviour on both road and track, one-up or fully loaded.

Scirocco

I have fond memories of the fuel-injected Scirocco Mk1 and Mk2 cars, having owned both after a brief flirtation with a Golf GTI 1600. When you drive a Scirocco, you sit in a fairly reclined position compared with the upright Golf, and, combined with the car's lower height and centre of gravity, this gives the impression of greater cornering stability. In real world terms, the skid-pan numbers of the two cars are not significantly different, but I have always felt a little braver cornering a Scirocco hard on a race circuit. The slight pitching motion induced by fast bumpy corners and caused by fairly soft rear dampers on all the Mk1 Golf and Scirocco 1 and 2 cars was felt least of all on Scirocco 1. Sitting higher up in the

The Scirocco Mk 2, left, is some years old now, but its pleasing shape and spritely performance endow it with more character than many newer designs. Right: an increasingly familiar sight as supply at last catches up with demand, the G60 Corrado is a true enthusiast's sports coupe and a worthy substitute for the now extinct 'entry level' Porsche.

Golf, you felt if more.

With more weight and overhang, the Mk2 Scirocco was less nimble than the first car. Even compared with the Golf Mk2, though, it is a quiet and refined car that is a pleasure to drive, especially in 112bhp form. It was not until I stepped back into a Scirocco Storm Mk1 that I realised how much more agile the original was. The older car was also much noisier, so if you do a lot of long distance work, the progress in refinement is a welcome thing.

The 16-valve Scirocco was only made in LHD form and sold in the UK to special order. I was lucky enough to have sampled the car in Germany in 1985 at the original press launch. With its lower strut brace and uprated springs and dampers, the car was a lot tauter than a Scirocco GTI and stopped better too, thanks to rear discs. When driven back-to-back with the Golf GTI 16V, though, it quickly became apparent that even these modifications could not begin to close the gap with the new-generation chassis. But for all that, the Scirocco 16V looks set to become a classic. Although the Scirocco is still in production, the 16V was the definitive factory car and the used-car market in Germany has already begun to underline that thinking.

Corrado

While in essence the Corrado has the floorpan and chassis from the Golf GTI Mk2, its rear axle design benefits from further technical progress made between the launch of Golf 2 in 1983 and the new Passat in 1987. The most significant feature is the passive rear-steer effect given by the special bushes that locate the trailing arms. The dynamic effect of rear wheel steering is better turn-in, better crosswind stability and more stable cornering. The Golf 2 is already very good when driven on the limit. It is initially hard to believe that the Corrado is significantly better, but those flexible bushings work very well and help to reduce understeer in fast corners. The reduced slip angles enhance cornering power and the Corrado's poise through corners sets new standards for front-wheel-drive hatchback cars.

The Corrado 16V is about 400lb heavier than the equivalent Golf GTI 16V. Thus you have to use the gears more to get up to speed, but superior aerodynamics mean that the car is quick once you have overcome inertia. The Euro-spec G60 offers performance more in line with the looks and chassis behaviour of the car, but with a penalty at the petrol pump as with any car that uses forced aspiration. The stiffer chassis creates even higher levels of handling and roadholding than the 16V, but the ride is firmer too. On smooth German roads this is fine, but on some broken British A-roads, the ride can become a little jittery.

In terms of build quality and refinement, the Corrado is superb. The car feels hewn from the solid. The driving position will be familiar to those who have owned Sciroccos or even a Porsche 924/944! The difference is that you can get two adults into the back seats of the Corrado and its ability to cruise happily at three-figure speeds makes it a real Grand Touring coupe.

10

Enthusiasts all

For many years, VWs have been enthusiasts' vehicles, witness the huge number of Beetle owners world-wide who make the effort to join VW Clubs and take part in organized events. But even the Beetle craze has been overtaken by the fanatical following of GTI owners. In Germany, almost every large town has a GTI Club and in both Holland and Germany there are Scirocco Clubs to cater for the VW coupe as well. Germany also has a few Golf Cabriolet Clubs for open air fans, and we will probably see Corrado Clubs starting up before long.

The Americans tend to integrate GTI enthusiasm into their normal VW Clubs but in Britain there is the GTI Drivers' Club and Club GTI while the hard-core South Africans have the very active GTi Club of SA. Club gatherings in all countries range from a monthly regional get-together for drinks and car talk to full-blown events at racing circuits. But the most spectacular GTI events occur at an international level. These tend to involve the VW importer and main dealers in the host country and are professionally organized, with technical lectures, exhibitions, film shows, sprints and slaloms.

The most famous of these giant GTI gatherings is the annual GTI Treffen (Convention) at Maria Worth on the edge of the Worthersee, a lake in Southern Austria. The first of these events in 1982 started off quite innocently as a small gathering of GTI enthusiasts. The meeting was a success and Volkswagen fuelled the fires by

The biggest and most well known GTI gathering is the annual GTI Treffen (convention) held each summer at Maria Worth on the edge of the Worthersee in Austria.

The next biggest gathering of GTIs in Europe is GTI International, organized by *VW Audi Car* magazine in Britain each May.

circulating details of the 1983 event to VW owners in Germany and Austria. Nearly 800 cars turned up for the second event. The scale of the event took it beyond club-level organization, and so Volkswagen took over the logistics in association with the local tourist board. The numbers of cars and people attending has been growing every year, and in 1985, the cars attending produced a six-mile long GTI traffic jam. Last year, with a record number of 1,160 cars at Maria Worth including a contingent from the British Club GTI, a monument to the GTI was carved out of stone by a group of craftsmen.

Another growing event is GTI International which is organised by *Volkswagen Audi Car*

magazine in the UK. In its second year in 1989, GTI International moved to the Transportation and Road Research Laboratory in Crowthorne, Berkshire, and under brilliant May sunshine, was a stunning success with 1,000 cars turning up over the weekend. The test establishment has a huge car park with room for slaloms and handling tests and there is a timed quarter-mile sprint, concours d'elegance, technical seminars, exhibitions and displays. In 1990 there will also be a sound-off competition for cars with customized audio systems. In 1989, several participants came over from Germany and as the fame of this event spreads, it could well equal the GTI Treffen in attendance in the years to come.

A fitting tribute to the greatest hot hatchback of them all: this GTI was carved from a block of stone by craftsmen at the 1989 GTI Treffen.

189

Some serious racing goes on within the activity programmes of GTI clubs in some parts of the world. The two Golfs and a Jetta locked in mortal combat here belong to members of the GTi Club of South Africa.

United Kingdom

GTI Drivers' Club
Michael Kingdon
160 Moore Road
Mapperley
Nottingham NG3 6EL

Club GTI
David Pipes
Cranhill Farmhouse
Cranhill Road
Street
Somerset BA16 0BZ

South Africa

GTi Club of SA
49 Dublin Street
Kenmare X4
1740 Krugersdorp

USA

Volkswagen Club of America
PO Box 154
North Aurora
IL 60542

Canada

Club Golf GTI
Gerard Gervais
CP 581
Sorel
Quebec
J3P 5N9

Australia

Golf GTI Club Victoria
John Rosengrave
13 Alexander Crescent
Ferntree Gulley
Victoria

Holland

GTI Club Holland
Peter van der Maden
Synagogestraat 7
NL-7001 AG Doetinchem

Denmark

Golf GTI Club Daenemark
Indusjtrivej 36
DK-4000 Roskilde

Sweden

Swedish Golf GTI Club North
Bo Holmvall
Professors V 48B
S-951 63 Lulea

Germany, Switzerland, Austria: these countries have numerous clubs organized on a regional basis and details may be obtained from the local VW distributors.

VW tuners, USA

Automotive Performance Systems/Neuspeed
1464 North Hundley Street
Anaheim
CA 92806

AutoTech Sport Tuning
3 Argonaut
Laguna Hills
CA 92656

Bellevue Motorsports
13500 Bel-Red Road #22
Bellevue
WA 98005

GMP Inc
710 Pressley Road
Charlotte
NC 28217

Power Haus Products Inc
19102 Ervin Lane
Santa Ana
CA 92705

Techtonics Tuning
1253 W La Cadena Drive
Riverside
CA 92501

VW tuners, United Kingdom

Autocavan
103 Lower Weybourne Lane
Badshot Lea
Farnham
Surrey GU9 9LG

BR Motorsport
8A Berrington Road
Sydenham Industrial Estate
Leamington Spa
Warwickshire CV31 1NB

GTi Engineering
Unit 9 Silverstone Circuit
Towcester
Northants NN12 8TN

Scotts of Sloane Square
(Agents for Oettinger conversions)
214-224 Pavilion Road
Sloane Square
London SW1X 0AN

Steiner Engineering Ltd
151 Stamford Brook Arches
Goldhawk Road
Chiswick
London W6 0TQ

VW tuners, South Africa

Erasmusrand Motors
425 Rigel Avenue
Erasmusrand
Pretoria

VW tuners, Germany

Abt Tuning
Oberwangerstr 16
D-8960 Kempten

Dannert Speedster Cabrio
Cronenberger Str 147B
D-5650 Solingen 1

Dennert Motorsport
Winkel Str 32
D-4100 Duisburg

Folger
Fohling 36
D-4790 Paderborn-Elsen

Hartmann Motorsport
Am Bergwald 39B
D-7000 Stuttgart 61

Hofele Design
Poststr 84
D-7322 Donzdorf

Kerscher Tuning
Falkenberger Str 17
D-8331 Rimbach-Dietring

KS Motorsport
Mulgaustr 187
D-4050 Monchengladbach

Kunkel Exklusiv
Postfach 31
D-8541 Buchenbach

Max-Moritz-Tuning
Max-Planck-Str 30
D-7410 Reutlingen

Oettinger GmbH Co KG
Max-Planck-Str 26
D-6382 Friedrichdorf

Nothelle
Cacilienstr 10-12
D-4330 Mulheim

Projektzwo Automobildesign
Fritz-Winter-Str 16
D-8918 Diessen

Rallye Sport Shop
Frankfurter Str 42
D-5210 Troisdorf 1

ASS
Rontgenstr 16
D-8047 Karlsfeld

WS Styling
Amerikastr 24
D-7488 Stetten A.K.M.

Steppan Autosport
Boschstr 6-8
D-4250 Bottrop 2

Rieger Tuning
Sternod 69
D-8333 Hebertsfelden

Zander Exklusiv Tuning
Liebigstr 33
D-6100 Darmstadt

Taifun Automobiltechnik
Spessartstr 42
D-6053 Obertshausen

Wochner Design
Robert Bosch Str 12-16
D-7778 Markdorf

K Treser GmbH
Kalbereschuttstr 8
D-8070 Ingolstadt

Vanetta GmbH
Morgensternstr 27
D-8070 Ingolstadt

Power Tech
Postfach 2073
D-5412 Ranbsbach-Baumbach

K.1 Motorentechnik
Moerser Str 214
D-4132 Kamp-Lintfort

Sorg Motorsport
Dieselstr 18
D-7068 Urbach

Speedster Ostermann
Jagdgrund 1
D-4530 Ibbenburen

Zastrow Car-Sport GmbH
Im Hammereisen 29-31
D-4193 Kranenburg

Vestatec
Karkstr 31
D-4353 Oer-Erkenschwick

Scmidt Motorsport
Am Steinacher Kreuz
D-8500 Nurnberg 90

Car Noblesse
Rebenroute 20
D-7000 Stuttgart 1

Happich GmbH
Postfach 100249
D-5600 Wuppertal 1

GK Auto Design
Theodor-Jansen-Str
D-6670 St Ingbert/Rohrbach

Wagner Automobiltechnik
Moltkestr 21
D-6620 Volklingen

VW tuners, Austria

Fosab
Bahnhofstr 63
A-4614 Marchtrenk

Foha
Unterhaidstr 15
A-4051 St Martin

MS Design
Huben 22
A-6444 Langenfeld